T0329629

Airport Competitiveness

Małgorzata Bednarczyk
Ewa Grabińska

Airport Competitiveness

Models and Assessment Methods

Jagiellonian University Press

Reviewer
prof. dr hab. Józef Sala

Cover illustration
Agata Bednarczyk

This volume has been published thanks to the financial support of the Department
of Management in Tourism, Faculty of Management and Social Communication
at the Jagiellonian University.

© Copyright by Małgorzata Bednarczyk, Ewa Grabińska & Jagiellonian University Press
    First edition, Krakow 2015
    All rights reserved

No part of this book may be reprinted or reproduced or utilized in any form or by any electronic,
mechanical, or other means, now known or here after invented, including photocopying and recording,
or in any information storage or retrieval system, without permission in writing from the publishers.

ISBN 978-83-233-4069-0
ISBN 978-83-233-9380-1 (e-book)

www.wuj.pl

Jagiellonian University Press
Editorial Offices: Michałowskiego 9/2, 31-126 Krakow
Phone: +48 12 663 23 80, +48 12 663 23 82, Fax: +48 12 663 23 83
Distribution: Phone: +48 12 631 01 97, Fax: +48 12 631 01 98
Cell Phone: + 48 506 006 674, e-mail: sprzedaz@wuj.pl
Bank: PEKAO SA, IBAN PL 80 1240 4722 1111 0000 4856 332

TABLE OF CONTENTS

LIST OF COMMON ABBREVIATIONS

ACI	Airports Council International
AEA	Association of European Airlines
AIP	Aeronautical Information Publication
APD	Air Passenger Duty
ASQ	Airport Services Quality
ATA	Air Transport Association of America
ATC	Air Traffic Control
Aviation Law	Act of 3 July 2002 – Aviation Law (Official Journal of 2006 No 100 item 696 with subsequent amendments)
BAA	British Airports Authority
CF	Cohesion Fund
Chicago Convention	The Convention on International Aviation signed in Chicago on 7 December 1944 (Official Journal of 1959 No 35 item 212 with subsequent amendments)
CoR	Committee of the Regions
CPL	Central Airport of Poland (*Centralny Port Lotniczy*)
Dz.U.	The Journal of Laws of the Republic of Poland (Dziennik Ustaw Rzeczpospolitej Polskiej)
EASA	European Aviation Safety Agency
EATCHIP	European Air Traffic Control Harmonization and Integration Program
EBI	European Investment Bank
EBRD	European Bank for Reconstruction and Development
EC	European Commission
ECAA	European Common Aviation Area
ECAC	European Civil Aviation Conference
EESC	European Economic and Social Committee
EMS	Environmental Management System
EP	European Parliament
ERA	European Regions Airlines Association
ERDF	European Regional Development Fund
ESF	European Social Fund
EU	European Union

Eurocontrol	European Organisation of Air Navigation Safety
Eurostat	European Statistical Office
GA	General Aviation – comprises all aviation traffic (private and commercial) with the exclusion of scheduled flights and military flights
GNSS	Global Navigation Satellite System – a type of radio navigation using radio waves from satellites
GUS	Central Statistical Office in Poland (Główny Urząd Statystyczny)
IACA	International Air Carrier Association
IAOPA	International Council of Aircraft Owner and Pilot Associations
IATA	International Air Transport Association
ICAO	International Civil Aviation Organization
ICCA	International Civil Airports Association
ILS	Instrument Landing System
ISO	International Organization for Standardization
JAA	Joint Aviation Authority
JAR	Joint Aviation Requirements
Konstytucja RP	The Polish Constitution (Konstytucja Rzeczypospolitej Polskiej) Act of 2 April 1997 – Official Journal No 78 item 483 with subsequent amendments
LCC	Low Cost Carriers
LF	Load Factor
MI	Polish Ministry of Infrastructure (Ministerstwo Infrastruktury)
MICE	Meetings – Incentives – Conventions – Exhibitions
MIS	Marketing Information Systems
MON	Polish Ministry of National Defence (Ministerstwo Obrony Narodowej)
M.P.	Official Gazette of the Republic of Poland (*Monitor Polski*)
MS	Polish Ministry of State Treasury (Ministerstwo Skarbu)
MTBiGM	Polish Ministry of Transport, Construction and Maritime Economy (Ministerstwo Transportu, Budownictwa i Gospodarki Morskiej)
MTiGM	Polish Ministry of Transport and Maritime Economy (Ministerstwo Transportu i Gospodarki Morskiej)
NIK	Supreme Audit Office (Najwyższa Izba Kontroli)
NSS	National Cohesion Strategy, National Strategic Reference Framework for the years 2007–2013 supporting Economic Growth and Employment. This document was approved by means of a decision by the EC and the Ministry of Regional Development, Warsaw, May 2007 (*Narodowa Strategia Spójności,*

	Narodowe Strategiczne Ramy Odniesienia 2007–2013 wspierające wzrost gospodarczy i zatrudnienie)
NTO	National Tourism Organization
OJEU	The Official Journal of the European Union
OOU	limited use areas (Obszary Ograniczonego Użytkowania)
Paris Convention	A convention on air navigation signed in Paris on 13 October 1919 (ratified in accordance with the Act of 23 September 1922) (Official Journal of 1929 No 6 item 54 and Official Journal of 1931 No 106 item 837)
pax	passengers, packs per person, packs → pax; number of passengers handled
PAŻP	Polish Air Navigation Services Agency (Polska Agencja Żeglugi Powietrznej)
PKm	passenger kilometre – the number of passengers carried multiplied by the total number of kilometres of the entire passenger connections network of a carrier
POIiŚ	Infrastructure and Environment Programme (Program Operacyjny Infrastruktura i Środowisko)
POT	Polish Tourism Organisation (Polska Organizacja Turystyczna)
PPL	The Polish Airports State Enterprise (Przedsiębiorstwo Państwowe „Porty Lotnicze")
PPP	public-private partnership
PRM	Passengers with Reduced Mobility
QMS	Quality Management System
ROT	Regional Tourist Organisation (Regionalna Organizacja Turystyczna)
SAD	Single Administrative Document
SES	Single European Sky
SLOT	Starts Landing Operation Time
SRK	The National Development Strategy (Strategia Rozwoju Kraju)
TEC	Treaty establishing the European Community (consolidated version Official Journal EU C 321E of 29.12.2006)
TEN-T	Trans-European Network – Transport
TEN-T EA	Trans-European Transport Network Executive Agency
TKm	ton-kilometre – the total number of tons of freight transported multiplied by the total number of kilometres of carrier freight services network
ULC	Civil Aviation Office (Urząd Lotnictwa Cywilnego)
Warsaw Convention	A convention unifying certain regulations on international air transportation, signed in Warsaw on 12 October 1929 (ratified in accordance with the Act of 28 January 1932) (Official Journal of 1929 No 18 item 113)

WTCC	World Travel and Tourism Council
ZRPL	Polish Association of Regional Airports (Związek Regionalnych Portów Lotniczych)

List of Polish airport codes

WAW	Warsaw Chopin Airport (Lotnisko Chopina w Warszawie)
BZG	Bydgoszcz Airport (Międzynarodowy Port Lotniczy im. Ignacego Jana Paderewskiego w Bydgoszczy)
GDN	Gdańsk Lech Wałęsa Airport (Port Lotniczy Gdańsk im. Lecha Wałęsy)
IEG	Zielona Góra-Babimost Airport (Port Lotniczy Zielona Góra-Babimost)
KRK	John Paul II International Airport Kraków-Balice (Międzynarodowy Port Lotniczy im. Jana Pawła II Kraków-Balice) (Kraków Airport im. Jana Pawła II)
KTW	Katowice International Airport (Międzynarodowy Port Lotniczy Katowice w Pyrzowicach)
LCJ	Łódź Airport (Port Lotniczy Łódź im. Władysława Reymonta)
LUZ	Lublin Airport (Port Lotniczy Lublin-Świdnik)
POZ	Poznań Airport (Port Lotniczy Poznań-Ławica im. Henryka Wieniawskiego)
RDO	Radom Airport (Port Lotniczy Radom-Sadków)
RZE	Rzeszów International Airport (Port Lotniczy Rzeszów-Jasionka)
SZY	Mazury Airport (Port Lotniczy Mazury)
SZZ	Szczecin Goleniów Airport (Port Lotniczy Szczecin-Goleniów im. NSZZ Solidarność)
WMI	Warsaw Modlin Airport (Mazowiecki Port Lotniczy Warszawa-Modlin)
WRO	Copernicus Airport Wrocław (Port Lotniczy Wrocław-Strachowice im. Mikołaja Kopernika)

One kilometre of motorway does not lead anywhere
– but one kilometre of runway enables connectivity
with the entire world

INTRODUCTION

Interpersonal contacts are one of the most essential values of the modern world. Despite the development of a variety of different forms of communication, a strong need for personal contact still remains. Hence the need for movement and travel. Air transport, as one of the areas of the economy, has been experiencing rapid development for many years now. One of the reasons for that is that this type of transport enables us to reach any point on Earth relatively quickly, conveniently and safely. Nevertheless, aviation shall not progress without sufficient infrastructure and its growth is therefore strictly related to the appearance of new airports and the development of existing ones.

The development of airports must be considered from the point of view of different entities (e.g. central authorities, regional governments, entrepreneurs, beneficiaries and citizens.) Furthermore one must not forget different groups of influencing factors (legal, institutional and environmental ones). Also, to maintain a variety of different views, it is vital for us to look at regional, national and international levels of reference.

As a result of the great impact of global economic trends (such as globalisation, liberalisation and deregulation) on the air transport market, the growth of airports is extremely dynamic and difficult to forecast. New technologies emerge, economic conditions change rapidly, and the awareness of environmental protection is now greater than ever. All these changes are taking place in times of great competition, as well as within certain financial constraints. Therefore, exploration of competitiveness is vital for all: the airport's owners and its management team. Competitiveness, at the same time, constitutes an interesting field of study and is a traditional area of activity of the world's greatest business consultancies.

The study of competitiveness is moreover vitally important for Polish regional airports, which, for historical reasons, have only started to develop in the last 20 years, and are currently beginning to strengthen their position on the aviation services market. It is crucial for regional airports to be able to face new challenges. Along with new opportunities, risk factors must also be taken into account. Poland's accession to the Organization for Economic Co-operation and Development (OECD), the European Union and the

Schengen Area, as well as other processes within the recent years, have had a great impact on the Polish aviation transport sector, which became an integral part of the European system. One must not forget that this sector constitutes a vital element of the economy and contributes to the technological and economic growth of the country.

Polish airports must operate in a highly competitive market, and only the right decisions by airport authorities based on relevant knowledge will allow them to stay on the market. Airport managers must face the issue of key factors for competitive advantage of regional airports, as well as the issue of strengthening their airport's competitive position on the passenger transport market. It is the aim of this monograph to address these challenges.

A structured collection of determinants (key factors) for the development of a regional airport is assumed to exist. The determinants shape an airport's competitive position and are essential to its growth. The evidence for the existence of such determinants is based on the analysis of selected factors of regional airport competitiveness. A model of competitiveness was created for practical use, with regard to managing regional airports in Poland.

The first chapter will characterise air transport in comparison to other types of transport. Next, its infrastructure will be described and the notions of *aerodrome* and *airport* will be defined in detail. Then a definition of the main object of this exploration, namely the *regional airport*, shall be created in accordance with binding legal norms in global transport. Furthermore, the current state of development of Polish airports, as compared to global and European transport infrastructure, shall be discussed. Air traffic data will be presented from a diachronic perspective.

The second chapter of this study shall be devoted to competitiveness of enterprises. Firstly, the essence, the concept, basic dimensions and relevance of competitive advantage will be presented. Next, the focus will be on competitiveness in transport, particularly in relation to the Polish air transport services market. The specifics of this market will be studied from the perspective of competitiveness. Moreover, the notion of substitute competitiveness will be presented. Finally, the rank of Polish airports in the competitive local and European markets will be discussed.

The third chapter will present a review of methods and tools for competitive analysis. These methods and tools will allow us to distinguish some characteristics that have essential impact on the competitive position of an airport. Moreover, the grounds for competitiveness and measures of competitiveness will be discussed.

Chapter four will cover the external and internal conditions concerning a regional airport's competitiveness. The first subchapter will depict external factors in relation to the macro-, meso- and microenvironments. Since one of the most vital elements increasing the competitiveness of an airport is the efficient use of (and expansion of) its catchment area, a structure of strategic players will be drafted, including a list of airports competing against particular Polish airports. The second subchapter will be devoted to internal competitiveness conditions. Special attention will be paid to the subject of skilful management of airports and, among others, to effective investment policy.

Finally, in the last, fifth chapter, an attempt will be made to empirically define the relevance of certain factors for the competitiveness of Polish airports in the area of passenger service. An econometric model estimated in a panel data trial with reference to 11 Polish airports in operation on the Polish passenger service market in the years 2007–2010 will constitute the basis for our findings.

The variety of source materials results from the necessity to analyse statistical data of air traffic volume based on figures drawn up by air transport organisations and other information pertaining to the operation of airports. The data was taken from Polish and European statistical yearbooks, as well as from domestic and global subject literature.[1] We also made use of a wide range of information and data available online.

---

[1] Information was taken from various statistical databases developed by Eurostat, the Civil Aviation Office, the Central Statistical Office in Poland and particular airports. Other sources used for reference include those from various entities such as international organisations (the Airports Council International, the International Air Transport Association) and entities, which are not directly related to air transport services (e.g. the Polish Institute of Tourism).

1. THE ESSENCE OF AIR TRANSPORT AND ITS SOCIO-ECONOMIC ROLE

The issue of competitiveness has only become essential for Polish airports relatively recently, as a result of on-going political and economic transformation. The transformation enabled the shift from central government control to market regulation.[2] Prior to exploration of competitiveness, we need to define the characteristics of air transport, and introduce the object of the research, namely the regional airport. Furthermore, we need to present the context of Polish regional airports development in relation to global air transport.

1.1. The essence of transport and its types

Transport itself is an activity, which aims to move something or someone from one place to another, over a distance, or to carry out a shipment. The term originates from the Latin word *transportare* (to carry, shift, move).[3] In accordance with the meaning of the word, transport is a shift (movement) from a starting point to a destination point. Economically speaking, the activity is a payable service provision that results in the movement of people and cargo, as well as the creation of auxiliary services that are directly connected thereto.[4]

---

[2] The issues in relation to pro-market system transformation in post communist countries of Central and Eastern Europe and other regions, initiated by a great breakthrough in the years 1989–1991, have recently became subject of broad social interest. Additionally, it became a subject of research, analysis and theoretical investigations of social sciences, mainly economic ones.

[3] The word is a combination of two terms with a distinctive meaning i.e. *trans* – through, to, outside of something, functioning as a part of many words e.g. transaction, transmission, transfusion, transformation, transfer, etc. The other term – *port* (Latin *portus*) denotes not only a berthing area (adequately protected and equipped) but also has a broader meaning of for example: aim, end, destination, place of anchorage. Source: K. Bentkowska-Senator, Z. Kordel, *Transport w turystyce*, Wydawnictwo Uczelniane WSG, Bydgoszcz 2008, p. 9.

[4] W. Rydzykowski, K. Wojewódzka-Król, *Transport. Problemy transportu w rozszerzonej UE*, Wydawnictwo Naukowe PWN, Warszawa 2009, p. 13.

Transport services constitute an intensifying factor for economic and social development in every nation.[5] Transport development tends to diminish the distance between markets, and it makes way for an increase in production. Moreover, it activates areas around the infrastructure, which, as a result, helps to increase employment. Transport facilitates the processes of industrialisation and urbanisation. Apart from servicing material production sectors, it also serves nonproduction sectors, such as health protection and education. Furthermore, it works for the populace by fulfilling their individual transport needs. In addition, it activates both socio-economic and cultural life, and it facilitates tourism growth.

It is assumed that the development of transport is impossible without economic growth, and vice versa: economic growth is impossible without transport development. Therefore, a strong connection exists between the development of both, which bears the characteristics of mutual growth.[6] Currently, it is not possible to substitute transport with any other activity.[7] It is thus impossible to reach rapid economic growth without a well-developed transport infrastructure. It is a civilisational necessity. The development of transport infrastructure (both the modernisation of existing infrastructure and the building of new infrastructure) is a catalyst for change, which results in a positive domino effect. The development of transport should take place in connection with other sectoral programmes.[8]

Transport is often subdivided – depending on what or who is being transported – into *passenger* and *goods transport*.[9] Considering the criterion of the environment in which the means of transport moves, we can divide the means of transportation into land transport, water transport and air transport. Depending on the type of transport being used, we may talk about car transport, rail transport, sea transport and air transport. From the point of view of the needs arising from contemporary socio-economic conditions, the most

---

[5] The share of transport in Polish GDP in 2010 was 6.5% (source: *Polska – podstawowe wielkości i wskaźniki w latach 1995–2010*, Ministerstwo Gospodarki, Warszawa 2011, p. 12, http://www.mg.gov.pl/files/upload/8436/Calosc%20Polska%20wielko%C5%9Bci%2 0pdf.pdf (access: 05.06.2013).

[6] A. Cholewa, *Koleje dużych prędkości w aspekcie rozwoju regionów Polski*, PKP PLK/RBF, seminar *High speed railways*, 14 November 2005.

[7] W. Rydzykowski, K. Wojewódzka-Król, *Transport. Problemy transportu w rozszerzonej UE*, op. cit., pp. 12–14.

[8] Broad analysis of the role of transport in economy may be found in T. Truskolaski, *Transport a dynamika wzrostu gospodarczego w południowo-wschodnich krajach bałtyckich*, Wydawnictwo Uniwersytetu w Białymstoku, Białystok 2006, pp. 13–54; M. Łatuszyńska, "Metody badania wpływu infrastruktury transportu na rozwój społeczno-ekonomiczny regionu," *Problemy Ekonomiki Transportu* 1, 2007, pp. 7–24; A. Domańska, *Wpływ infrastruktury transportu na rozwój regionalny*, Wydawnictwo Naukowe PWN, Warszawa 2006.

[9] However, it must be remembered that using the words as mutually exclusive is not correct as not all persons using transport are passengers and not all load is a cargo.

beneficial transport is by air.[10] This is due to time of transfer, cost, reliability, transport capability, spatial accessibility and safety. Moreover, this type of transport is a strong medium for technological and organisational development, and it is a pioneering field with regard to the introduction of Information Technology tools, new technologies and communication techniques.

1.2. The origin and specificity of air transportation

Although the concept of using the air to move has been close to humankind for many decades,[11] it is considered as a fact that the history of air transport goes back only one century. On the 17th of December 1903, the brothers Wilbur and Orville Wright made their first flight in a Chanute biplane powered by an internal combustion engine[12] in Kitty Hawk. This was the first reported passenger journey with an aircraft heavier than air. From this moment on, air transport has developed rapidly, particularly in the United States. Air transport started to gain significance at the end of the 1950s (mainly due to intercontinental flights). In the following years, air transport came to more or less dominate intercontinental travel. In Poland, civilian air transport was initiated by the first passenger flight from Poznań to Warsaw in 1919. In 1923, regular flights from Warsaw to Gdańsk and Lviv were introduced, and Polish Airlines (Polskie Linie Lotnicze LOT) company was founded in 1929. Air transport infrastructure started to develop, and new airports were created in Warsaw, Kraków and other cities.[13]

The term *air transport*, used to define transport by air with the use of a means of transport referred to as an aircraft, shall be construed as the intentional movement of people and cargos in airspace, distinguished from other activities in technical, organisational and economic relations.[14]

---

[10] At this point we can provisionally mention that function assessment of a branch of transport should be carried out in accordance with the following criteria: time of transport, cost, reliability, transport capacity, spatial availability and safety.

[11] In 1250, Roger Bacon wrote on possibilities of human flying, and in the fifteenth century Leonardo Da Vinci made first drafts of a parachute, an ornithopter and a helicopter.

[12] Wright Flyer, built by the Wright brothers, is considered to be the first plane that made a flight on its own. The first flight lasted 33 seconds with 36.5 metres distance covered. On the same day, the Wright brothers made three more flights covering the distance of 270 metres, with the duration of the longest flight – 59 seconds.

[13] More detailed data on the genesis and history of aviation transport in the world and in Poland may be found in E. Grabińska, *Determinanty konkurencyjności regionalnego portu lotniczego*, Uniwersytet Jagielloński, Kraków 2014 (PhD Thesis), annex, p. 11.

[14] Source: M. Żylicz, *Międzynarodowy obrót lotniczy. Zagadnienia ekonomiczno-prawne*, Wydawnictwa Komunikacji i Łączności, Warszawa 1972, p. 25. The notion is also defined in European documentation, where *air transport* refers to aircraft transport of passengers, luggage, cargo and mail, separately or jointly, offered to public for remuneration or by way of lease

The air transport market comprises factors that condition air travel and, therefore, both the providers and the recipients of air services[15] may be classified in different ways.[16] With reference to the distance of the journey, the following market segments are distinguished: short distance markets (up to 1,000 km), medium distance markets (1,000-3,000 kilometres) and long distance markets (over 3,000 kilometres). Depending on their functions, the following types of aviation may be distinguished: civil aviation, military aviation, sports aviation, marine aviation, industrial aviation, transport aviation and medical aviation. It is essential to further investigate **transport aviation,** which aims to transport people, goods and mail in an organised way. This type of transport is carried out by airlines (air carriers). Air transport may be divided into regular lines and non-regular ones (charter lines).

Air travel is an integral part of the global world in the 21st century. At present, passenger transport constitutes over 85% of world air transport.[17] It is estimated that all airlines around the world carry over a few billion passengers over a distance of tens of millions of kilometres.[18] World air transport provides 56.6 million jobs and its share in the global GDP is 3.5%, which amounts to 2.2 billion dollars.[19]

which – to avoid uncertainty – consists of scheduled (regular) and non-scheduled (irregular) transport as well as cargo transport solely. Source: article 1 item 3 of the agreement on Joint Aviation Area by and between the European Union, Member States and the Republic of Moldova, *Official Journal of the European Union,* L 292/3, 20.10.2012, http://eur-lex.europa.eu/LexUriServ/LexUriServ.do?uri=OJ:L:2012:292:0003:0037: PL:PDF (access: 20.11.2013).

[15] A. Ruciński, *Porty lotnicze wobec polityki otwartego nieba,* Fundacja Rozwoju Uniwersytetu Gdańskiego, Gdańsk 2008, p. 22.

[16] Detailed classification of air service market, see E. Grabińska, *Determinanty konkurencyjności,* op. cit., annex, p. 39.

[17] A. Ruciński, *Porty lotnicze wobec polityki otwartego nieba,* op. cit., p. 37.

[18] According to ACI, in 2006, number of passengers in world regular transport was over 4.2 billion, and in 2009 the number was over 4.4 billion. In 2011 passenger air transport increased by 4.9%, in comparison with the previous year, and amounted to 4.9312. As the number of people flying increased, the freight transport (cargo) decreased by 0.1% and amounted to 8.67 billion. The decrease was a result of unstable economic situation. Source: http://centreforaviation.com/news/aci-reports-49-rise-in-passenger-numbers-in-2011-cargo-flat-148074 (access: 20.11.2013).

[19] Currently, 1568 commercial airlines, 3846 commercial airports, 192 air traffic control services and 23,844 airplanes operate. Out of 56.6 million workplaces supported by air transport, 8.4 million people are directly employed in the sector, 9.3 million are employed by air industry suppliers and 4.4 million workplaces result from the expenses of air transport workers (if we add the tourism sector, there are 34.5 million workplaces more.) The European industry of air transport provides 8.7 million workplaces and 749 billion USD in European GDP – data of 2010. Source: ATAG, *Aviation Benefits beyond Borders,* March 2012, acquired from http://www.aviationbenefits- beyondborders.org/download-abbb-report (access: 20.11.2013).

1.3. Infrastructure in air transportation

It is no secret that transport cannot develop without the appropriate infrastructure. The term **transport infrastructure** is referred to as a transportation network used by a given means of transport during movement and rest.[20] This infrastructure requires relatively large investments. However, one should take into account that the infrastructural elements are in use for a long time.

Transport infrastructure is most commonly divided into line and point infrastructure.[21] Line infrastructure means all routes on which the means of transport shall move. In air transport, natural air passages called air corridors constitute the main element of line infrastructure. It is vital that the air space only gains infrastructural features when appropriate leading devices are installed such as: radars, communication radio stations, navigation radio stations, and means of satellite communications. These devices, along with the buildings in which they are located, constitute the equipment of line infrastructure in air transport.[22]

For all flight phases, one should consider not only the flight itself, but also the moment of landing. Therefore, the **point infrastructure system** in air transport basically consists of an airspace control system and flight control system (comprising a movement control system, radar stations, radio communications system between pilots and flight controllers and communications between control centres and airports.) The order in which the points of air transport were listed refers to the historic development of the term, and nowadays, it applies to the scope of services offered by the infrastructure points.

The above definitions are determined by the Aviation Law (Journal of Laws of the Republic of Poland, 2006, no. 100, item 696 with subsequent amendments). Hence an **airdrome** is primarily an area designated on land, water or another surface, which is either wholly or partially designed for take offs, landings and taxiing (movement of aircraft on the ground). They are registered in the airdrome register (art. 2 clause 5 of the Aviation Law). In contrast, an **airport** also comprises permanent buildings and technical equipment (art. 2 clause 4 of the Aviation Law).[23]

Airports are subdivided into those for public use, and those for exclusive use. Airports feature runways, control towers, lighting systems, radars and

---

[20] Transport infrastructure comprises all objects and stationary equipment located permanently and enabling operations. Source: J. Neider, *Transport międzynarodowy*, Polskie Wydawnictwo Ekonomiczne, Warszawa 2008, p. 2.

[21] P. Rosik, M. Szuster, *Rozbudowa infrastruktury transportowej a gospodarka regionów*, Wydawnictwo Politechniki Poznańskiej, Poznań 2008, p. 8.

[22] Compare E. Mendyk, *Ekonomika i organizacja transportu*, Wyższa Szkoła Logistyki, Poznań 2002, p. 70.

[23] A. Ruciński, *Porty lotnicze wobec polityki otwartego nieba*, op. cit., p. 135.

signal systems which all enable the handling of planes day and night, as well as during severe weather conditions, such as fog, snow and rain. Remaining parts of an airport include hangars, warehouses, terminals, customs and passport control areas, along with other related areas. One should note that airports have recently been undergoing major organisational changes, both with regard to their space and function. Some time ago, airports were merely seen as places for planes to take off and land.[24] However, the last few decades have seen their transformation into something new. They now offer a variety of services from basic ones, such as shops and restaurants, to more sophisticated ones, like banks, spas, karaoke bars and golf courts, among others.

An **airport** is a strategic object of air transport point infrastructure. It is considered to be an aerodrome with buildings, equipment and ground service suitable for air transport (this includes transporting passengers, luggage, goods and mail).[25] As a result, we may distinguish between two types of transportation airports, namely passenger airports and cargo airports (depending on the buildings and equipment they possess). However, most airports perform both functions at the same time.

The main scope of aiports' activity is ground passenger and cargo service, as well as the provision of material, technical and navigational backup for aircraft taking off and landing there.[26]

One may distinguish between state-owned airports,[27] airports that are owned by the local government, and private airports. This classification is closely related to another: central, regional and local.[28] The criteria involved are as follows: the amount of goods/people being transported (large airports – *hubs*, medium-sized airports [regional], small airports);[29] types of transport handled (passenger, cargo); number of air operations (take-offs

---

[24] Expansion of air transport point infrastructure was necessary due to technological changes that occurred in line infrastructure, e.g. a major change in airport infrastructure (increased capacity of airports – particularly the demand to build more spacious terminals – was facilitated by the appearance of Boeing 707 in 1955 (first series produced jet craft passenger airplane that could board about 200 passengers.) It is vitally important for airports to possess runways with proper parameters – for Boeing 737 the runway must be at least 2100 metres long.

[25] The differences between the terms *aerodrome* and *airport* are vague and both words are used freely in different contexts. Source: Organizacja Międzynarodowego Lotnictwa Cywilnego [ICAO], *Podręcznik służb lotniskowych*, Doc 9137-AN/898, http://brama.pwsz.chelm.pl:2222/cgi-bin/libraopac.dll? bcd&sID=0&hID=54601&lTyp=1 (access: 15.01.2014).

[26] A detailed investigation on the subject is carried out hereinafter.

[27] Rozporządzenie Ministra Infrastruktury z dnia 30 kwietnia 2004 r. w sprawie klasyfikacji lotnisk i rejestru lotnisk cywilnych, Dz.U. z 2004 r., nr 122, poz. 1273.

[28] J. Neider, *Transport międzynarodowy*, op. cit., p. 94.

[29] It is not easy to precisely state which airports are large and which are small, and, particularly in the European Union, various authorities classify them differently. However, classification is necessary in terms of the State aid for airports.

and landings); and airport function (e.g. international long-, medium- or short-distance transport).

All airports, aerodromes and other places adapted for take-offs and landings may also be classified according to the following criteria (among others):

- airport reference code number – an alphanumeric designation with reference to the length and width of the airport's runway, as well as the types of aircraft that may be handled on the latter;[30]
- function – independent airports, major airports, auxiliary airports;
- types of aircraft to be operated at the airport – planes, helicopters, gliders, seaplanes;
- availability to operators – of public or exclusive use;
- landing categories – nongovernment, government, precise (landing categories I, II, III – A, B, C), imprecise.

1.4. The notion of the regional airport

The abundance of criteria for airports makes it difficult to state clearly which airdromes (or airports) may be designated as **regional airports**.

European Union documents do not give one precise definition of an airport. They only give the following explanation: *an airport is a civil port where over fifty thousand operations (arrivals and departures) take place a year.*[31] Additionally, regulation No 2408/92 defines an airport as follows: *every area open for operations of air trade transport.* There is no one clear definition of particular types of airports, as various European institutions classify them in a similar (however, not identical) manner.

In 1996, the European Council (further referred to as the EC) and the European Parliament (hereinafter EP) jointly issued a decision No 1692/96/EC comprising the division of airports into three categories (Table 1). Subsequently, in the year 2002, the Committee of the Regions (hereinafter CoR) provided the following distinction of five categories (Table 2).

---

[30] E. Zabłocki, *Lotnictwo cywilne. Lotnictwo służb porządku publicznego*, Akademia Obrony Narodowej, Warszawa 2006, p. 17.

[31] J. Neider, *Transport międzynarodowy [International transport]*, op. cit., p. 91.

Table 1. Division of airports into three categories

The classification of airports according to decision No 1692/96/EC	
International communication points	5 million and more passenger flights per year
Community communication points	1 to 5 million passenger flights per year
Airports constituting regional nodal points and access points	250,000 to 1 million passenger flights per year

Source: adapted from G. Zając, *Wspólna polityka lotnicza Unii Europejskiej*, Państwowa Wyższa Szkoła Wschodnioeuropejska w Przemyślu, Przemyśl 2009, p. 107; after: Decision No 1692/96 of EP and the Council of 23 July 1996 on the Community guidelines for the development of the trans-European transport network.

Table 2. Division of airports into five categories

The classification of airports – attachment 1 CoR 393/2003		
Category A	Large transfer hubs	handling over 25 million passengers (about 35% of all aviation transport in the EU – 4 airports)
Category B	National airports	handling 5 to 10 million passengers (about 35% of all aviation transport in the EU – 16 airports)
Category C	Airports	handling 5 to 10 million passengers (about 14% of all aviation transport in the EU – 15 airports)
Category D	Airports	handling 1 to 5 million passengers (about 17% of all aviation transport in the EU – 57 airports)
Category E	Airports	handling 200,000 to 1 million passengers (about 4% of all aviation transport in the EU – 67 airports)

Source: adapted from G. Zając, *Wspólna polityka lotnicza Unii Europejskiej*, op. cit., p. 108; after: The Outlook Opinion of the Committee of the Regions of 2 July 2003 on the capacity of regional airports (CoR 393/2003), attachment No 3.

Although the airports in the C, D and E categories are classified as regional, the Committee of the Regions decided that the range was too broad and created a five-category classification based on the following criteria: the intensity and distribution of traffic; functionality; the geographical location and specialisation of airports; or the combinations of all functions (Table 3).

Table 3. Classification of airports according to The Committee of the Regions

The criteria for the classification of airports according to the Committee of the Regions		
A		Hub airports
A	hubs	handling over 25 million passengers or international or intercontinental communication points with high traffic
B		National airports
B	national airports	handling over 25 million passengers or international or intercontinental communication points with relatively high traffic
C		Regional airports: operating within European transport networks, potential intermodal centres
C1	specialised airports	specialisation in cargo transport or low-cost carriers' scheduled passenger flights
C2	relief airports	specialisation in traffic relief at hubs secondary airports
C3	system airports	airports as part of a system of private or state ownership
D		Regional airports: operating within regional networks, and of a more regional nature
D1	periphery airports	airports located further from the main business, political and scientific centres or hubs
D2	charter airports	specialisation in charter flights
E		Other regional and local airports (existing when economic benefits are higher than the costs)
E1	independent regional airports	handling over 200,000 passengers
E2	independent local airports	handling over 200,000 passengers

Source: adapted from G. Zając, *Wspólna polityka lotnicza Unii Europejskiej*, op. cit., p. 108; after: The Outlook opinion of the Committee of Regions of 2 July 2003 on the capacity of regional airports (CoR 393/2003), annex 3.

The European Union decided to create its own classification of airports and add types of airports that were not included in earlier classifications (Table 4 and Table 5).

Table 4. Division of airports into four categories (Decision 1692/96/EC)

Division of airports according to the European Commission		
Category A	large community airports	passenger flights volume – less than 10 million a year
Category B	national airports	passenger flights volume – 5 to 10 million a year
Category C	large regional airports	passenger flights volume – 1 to 5 million a year
Category D	small regional airports	passenger flights volume – less than 1 million a year

Source: adapted from G. Zając, *Wspólna polityka lotnicza Unii Europejskiej*, op. cit., p. 108; after: The Outlook opinion of the Committee of Regions of 2 July 2003 on the capacity of regional airports (CoR 393/2003), annex 3.

Table 5. Classification of Polish airports according to the EER Systems Corporation

Airport category	Airport definition
International	International airports constituting arrival and departure ports for scheduled and non-scheduled international flights that provide full services of inspection, customs and immigration, as well as enable contact with local authorities. The airports must comply with all requirements and recommendations of the ICAO, as well as the policies published in the AIP (*Aeronautical Information Publication*).
Regional	Large regional airports handling scheduled and non-scheduled flights for international regional transport. Other services include: on-demand flights; local private aircraft operations; air cargo transport and restricted international flights requiring earlier notification. Regional airports may also serve as alternative airports (supplementary airports) for international airports.
Secondary	Secondary airports serving the small industry and tourist sector or acting as trade centres. Access to airports is restricted to on-demand and private aircraft, as well as aircraft serving business people and small-scale transport. Secondary airports generally do not serve scheduled flights. They have a hardened runway.
General aviation	General aviation airports handling non-scheduled general aviation flights and forced landing operations of general aviation aircraft. Additionally, they serve as training or sports activity areas. They do not have a hardened runway.

Source: adapted from *Transport* edited by W. Rydzykowski, K. Wojewódzka-Król, *Transport. Problemy transportu w rozszerzonej UE*, Wydawnictwo Naukowe PWN, Warszawa 2009, p. 150; after: *Plan generalny rozwoju i programu inwestycyjnego polskiego lotnictwa cywilnego. Streszczenie wykonawcze*, EER Systems Corporation, Vienna, Virginia 1992.

The above classification of airports is especially important with regard to the EU's policy of financial support for the development of European airports, as well as its policy of awarding grants and subsidies.

1.5. Polish regional airports on the global aviation map

According to ACI report,[32] in the year 2010 there were 1318 airports in operation. For many years, as well as since the base year 2010, the dynamics of air transport has been accelerating. In 2013 there was a rise in the number of passengers served in the market of air transport services to the level of 5682 passenger/km, and the number of carried passengers exceeded 3 billion people. In the next year, 2014, the volume of passengers/km amounted to 6146 (an increase by 5.8%), and the number of passengers exceeded 3.3 billion people.

The share of individual regions of the world in the air transport market varies. In the base year 2010, North American airports dominated with 30% of carried passengers, and 32% of transported cargo. Europe reached 30% and 20% respectively, while the Asia – Pacific region accounted for 26% and 35% respectively. The shares of the other three regions are relatively insignificant. South and Latin America accounted for 8% and 5% respectively. The Middle East and North Africa accounted for 4% and 7% respectively. Africa (excluding North African countries) accounted for 3% and 2% respectively. In 2014, the percentage of carried passengers and transported cargo for geographical regions was the following: North America (25.4% and 25.2%), Europe (26.4% and 27%), Asia and the Pacific (33.5% and 31.4%), South and Latin America (7.3% and 5.2%) and Africa (2.2% and 2.2%).

The following connections play the biggest role in global aviation: transatlantic connections between Western Europe and North America; connections between the USA and Central and South American countries (as well as with Japan) and also connections between Western Europe and the Middle East, India, Japan and Australia.

According to the ACI, the thirty biggest airports in terms of the number of passengers handled in 2010 are as follows: 13 airports in North America (the USA), 9 airports in Asia and Pacific (China, Japan, Thailand, Singapore and Australia), 7 airports in Europe (Great Britain, France, Germany, Spain and Italy) and 1 airport in the Middle East (United Arab Emirates). In 2010, the leader in the number of passengers handled was an American airport of Atlanta-Hartsfield (89 million). Beijing airport (almost 74 million passengers) was second. Chicago O'Hare Airport (almost 67 million passengers) came in

---

[32] The ACI organisation (Airports Council International) consociates the 573 biggest airports and the authorities of 1650 airports operating in 178 countries and regions.

third. In 2014, the following airports maintained their position: the Atlanta Airport (96 million passengers) and Beijing Airport (86 million passengers), while the third position was occupied by Kuala Lumpur Airport (83 million passengers).

In 2010, the world's biggest airline with regard to the number of passengers handled was Delta Air Lines (162.6 million) and the other leading airlines were as follows: United Airlines (145.6 million) and Southwest Airlines (130.9 million). The Polish carrier PLL LOT, with 4.3 million passengers, occupied the 114th place on the list. According to the 2014 statistics, the first place was taken by the American Airlines Group (a merger of American Airlines and US Airways), and the subsequent places belong to United Airlines and Delta Airlines.[33]

Due to the liberalisation processes concerning the entire aviation industry, which took place at the beginning of the 1990s, European airports have undergone rapid development. Nevertheless, airports in our continent are poorly located and this constitutes an infrastructural barrier for aviation carriers. This gives rise to, for example, problems with maintaining the right level of capacity and, despite modernisation and expansion, these airports cannot meet the constantly growing demand for flights with the due service.

It is estimated that there are over 3100 airports located in the EU.[34] However, most of them are not actively used or belong to military aviation. Only 350 are active passenger airports, which belong to or are used by civil aviation. EU countries control the biggest share of Europe's aviation. In 2010, the airports of 27 EU Member States handled about 750 million passengers altogether and the average increase in 2007–2010 was 3.0%.[35] The structural location of passenger transport in EU countries is mainly concentrated in large western European countries, which share 70% of the market. British airports handled 192.8 million passengers (18.2%), German airports 166.1 million (15.6%), Spanish airports 153.3 million (14.4%), French airports 122.8 million (11.6%) and Italian airports 109 million passengers (10.3%).[36]

---

[33] The pKm index, which measures the distance covered by a passenger, confirms the dominance of American carriers; American Airlines Group with first place in 2014 [352 in billion pKm], United Airlines with second place [330 billion pKm], Delta Airlines with third place [326 billion pKm]. *Rynek lotniczy 2015: Air Transport Market 2015*, developed by D. Tłoczyński, Instytut Turystyki w Warszawie, "Wiadomości Turystyczne," Warszawa 2015.

[34] According to ACI statistics, in the year 2010, 454 airports were operating in 46 European countries (including the former USSR, Greenland and Turkey.) Most of them were in France, Spain, Russia, Greece and Great Britain. In total, 1,450 million of passengers were handled (30.2% of the global number,) 17.5 million tons of cargo transported (20.65%) and 18 million take-offs and landings took place.

[35] The data is quoted from Eurostat: http://epp.eurostat.ec.europa.eu/statistics_explained/index.php/ Passenger_transport_statistics (access: 20.10.2014).

[36] As above.

In 2014, an increase of passenger traffic in Europe was noted up to 871 million, with the following share of passengers served in: Britain (220 million), Germany (186 million), Spain (165 million), France (141 million), and Italy (121 million).

Poland handled 18.3 million passengers (1.7% of the total) in 2010, which gave it the 14th place in the European Union. Similar results were achieved by smaller western European countries, such as Austria, Ireland and Belgium (22–23 million passengers) and central European countries (The Czech Republic, Romania, Hungary), which handled 8–12 million passengers.[37] In 2014, Poland handled 25.7 million passengers, whereas, e.g. Austria served 26.3 million, Ireland 26.3 million, Belgium 28.7 million; and the countries in Central Europe, i.e. The Czech Republic (12 million), Romania (10 million), and Hungary (9 million).

In 2010, the airports that handled the biggest number of passengers were as follows: London Heathrow (65.7 million passengers), Paris Charles de Gaulle (57.9 million) and Frankfurt/Main (52.6 million). These airports were also among the top ten in the world in terms of the numbers of passengers served. For comparison, the biggest Polish passenger airport, Warsaw (WAW), handled about 7 times fewer passengers (8.7 million) than the leader in the ranking. In subsequent years, there was an increase in handled transportation traffic, however, London Heathrow with 73.4 million passengers, Paris Charles de Gaulle with 63.8 million, and Frankfurt/Main with 59.5 million still remain the European leaders. Warsaw airport took the 29th place, and handled 10.6 million passengers.

The current apportionment and location of airports in Poland is a result of geopolitical processes. The network of airports began to expand vigorously before World War II, and the first Polish airports were strongly associated with military activity. After the war, most airports were used exclusively for military purposes, and only later were they made available for civilian use. Until the 1990s, the capital's airport (Warszawa-Okęcie) was dominant, while other airports played only a minor role. Warsaw airport was a hub for Poland and, for many years, it had a major share in Polish passenger transport. At present, this role is diminishing as other airports gain significance in different regions. At one time, the capital airport was even expected to close due to loss of capacity (this did not happen).

After the liberalisation of airport services market in 2004, the regional airports, mainly those located in big cities, started to expand by introducing

---

[37] In 2007–2010, Poland noted a major average increase in the number of passengers as compared to other European countries. Poland came 7th in the EU (next to Austria and Italy, which showed average increases of 7.9% and 7.1% respectively). The average increase of the number for the entire EU was 3.0% at the time.

international flights, usually by "cheap" airlines (Low Cost Carriers). Undoubtedly, the growth of the regional airports largely results from the operation of low cost airlines such as EasyJet, Ryanair, SkyEurope, Centralwings and Wizz Air.

Regular air transport is currently carried out at several Polish airports, which include Warszawa-Okęcie (WAW) as a central airport, and the following regional airports: Bydgoszcz-Szwederowo (BZG); Gdańsk-Rębiechowo (GDN); Katowice-Pyrzowice (KTW); Kraków-Balice (KRK); Łódź-Lublinek (LCJ); Poznań-Ławica (POZ); Rzeszów-Jasionka (RZE); Szczecin-Goleniów (SZZ); Wrocław-Strachowice (WRO); Zielona Góra-Babimost (IEG); Warszawa-Modlin (WMI); Lublin-Świdnik (LUZ) and Radom-Sadków (RDO). Local airports (such as sports airports or aeroclubs, military airports and private airports) are also registered (see: Drawing 1).[38]

Out of all the transport airports, three are located practically inside cities (WAW, POZ, LCJ), which results in various limitations.[39] The Gdańsk Lech Wałęsa Airport was built as a civilian airport in 1974. It was designed and built with too little forethought.[40] Other airports, being former military airports,[41] required modernisation. At the commencement of their operation, these airports lacked the infrastructure that would allow big increases in air traffic. This involved: terminals, parking areas for airplanes, rapid exit ways and approach systems equipment, as well as the right length and carrying capacity parameters of runways.

The regional network of connections reflects economic, historical and tourist movements. The popularity of many connections is a result of many factors, such as new job markets for Polish citizens, or the country of origin of foreign investors in a given region.[42] As a rule, regional airports combine

---

[38] It is presumed that one central airport, over a dozen regional airports and over 100 local airports existed in Poland in the examined period. Moreover, it should be pointed out that the activity of Polish airport Szczytno-Szymany (code: IATA: SZY, code: ICAO: EPSY) is currently suspended. However, construction work is ongoing and the airport is due to reopen in 2016. Furthermore, construction of Gdynia-Kosakowo Airport (Gdynia-Oksywie, Gdynia-Babie Doły) has been stopped. Nevertheless, the construction of the following airports is planned in Poland: Central Polish Airport in Warsaw, Białystok-Saniki Airport, Kielce-Obice Airport, Nowy Sącz-Stary Sącz Airport.

[39] The implementation of the requirements of Annex 14 of The Chicago Convention is mainly restricted due to the geometry of the old part of DS (vertical systems) and already existing structures in the approaching area.

[40] The terminal of the airport was built too close to the taxiway and, moreover, it is not possible to add more modules to the terminal.

[41] The airports were built for light airplanes (a military plane weights a few tons, while a transport plane weights several dozen tons.) They were later modernised to take civilian planes and are continually being expanded and equipped with adequate navigation systems.

[42] For example, on the one hand in the Romanian air transport network, apart from connections with neighbouring countries, connections to Italian cities dominate, which reflects

Drawing 1. Location of Polish airports

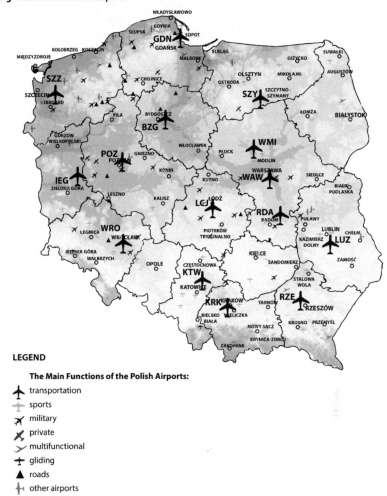

LEGEND

The Main Functions of the Polish Airports:

✈ transportation
✦ sports
✈ military
✗ private
⤳ multifunctional
✚ gliding
▲ roads
⊬ other airports

Source: own study.

many functions by not only handling travel of a typically tourism-related nature – both group travel (mainly charter flights) and individual travel (mainly flights by low cost airlines, for instance, from/to airports near popular tourist destinations)[43] – but also by handling transport for business, for work purposes or meeting family and friends.

the traditional Italian-Romanian links. On the other hand, a relatively small number of airports offer (and have offered) connections to Russia or Ukraine, though these connections are popular from the Czech Republic, Romania and Bulgaria.

[43] We may distinguish airports that mainly service outbound tourism and organised group tourism (e.g. Ostrava). They mostly offer charter flights to the South of Europe. A dif-

The capital's airport still dominates today, and it handles over three times more passengers than one of the biggest regional airports, namely John Paul II International Airport in Kraków-Balice. Although the connections to and from Warsaw still constitute a vital element of air traffic, the position of Okęcie as a hub diminishes every year.[44] Polish regional airports are gradually beginning to play a bigger role. At present, the total share of regional airports in passenger traffic amounts to 60%. Warsaw still dominates in cargo transport, although the share of the regional airports in Katowice and Wrocław is increasing.

An unprecedented increase in the total number of passengers handled in Poland took place in 2004. The number of passengers amounted to 8.9 million and was more than 25% higher than in 2003 (the increase in 2003 was 8% compared to 3.8% in 2002.) The year 2004 was particularly important for Polish aviation when, along with Poland's accession to the EU, new opportunities arose, including those for the aviation sector. Airlines were able to develop new connections. Moreover, the introduction of new regulations opened new possibilities for growth, particularly for Polish regional airports.[45] The number of passengers handled has risen drastically, as the Polish market was among the most rapidly developing markets in the world, comparable to the Chinese market. The year 2004 initiated a four-year period of big increases in Polish market figures. However, the crisis year of 2009 brought negative dynamics for most airports. The biggest decrease was experienced by the IEG regional airport (–36.3%). Only two regional airports saw an increase in the number of passengers (though it was much smaller than in previous years), namely RZE (18.4%) and BZG (7.7%). In 2010, most airports saw an increase in the number of passengers, with the highest increases at IEG (27.1%) and WRO regional airports (21.0%). Decreases were observed at SZZ (–4.7%) and BZG (–4.5%). In 2010 Polish airports handled 20.4 million passengers, including 8.6 million at WAW airport, 2.8 million at KRK airport, and 2.3

---

ferent group of airports consists of those servicing inbound tourism. They often have a small amount of scheduled flights (e.g. Karlove Vary, Burgas, Balaton). Additionally, these airports show big seasonal differences as to the number of passengers handled.

[44] The role of hubs for connections to Poland has been taken over by foreign airports, e.g. London-Stansted, which offers connections to most regional airports in Poland, and German airports, such as Frankfurt and Munich. As a result of the operation of the new Berlin Airport, the position of Warsaw Airport as a hub for passengers from Poland and border areas may be seriously threatened in the future.

[45] Polish airports are constantly getting new carriers in order to expand the connections network, as well as to increase passenger traffic. New carriers have started to operate, particularly low cost carriers like EasyJet, SkyEurope and Ryanair (among others). Source: D. Tłoczyński, "Skutki liberalizacji rynku usług transportu lotniczego dla regionalnych portów lotniczych" [in:] *Transport morski i lotniczy w obsłudze ruchu pasażerskiego*, ed. H. Salmonowicz, Wydawnictwo Naukowe Uniwersytetu Szczecińskiego, Szczecin 2005.

million at KTW airport. In subsequent years there was a stable growth in the number of passengers served, and in 2014 that number rose to 27.6 million passengers, including 38% (10.5 million) at WAW airport, 13.7 (3.8 million) at KRK airport, and 9.6% (2.6 million) at KTW airport.

Polish airports, as compared to airports in other parts of the world, are not extensive and rank relatively low in various rankings. In 2014 Poland ranked 14th among 28 European countries in terms of the number of passengers handled. Nevertheless, in the light of current predictions and predominant tendencies, the prospects for the development of Polish airports look good.

2. SIGNIFICANCE OF COMPETITIVENESS IN AIR TRANSPORTATION

A condition necessary for competition to exist as an economic phenomenon is a free-market economy. Competition itself creates foundation for market processes. It also regulates the behaviour of all entities existing on the market. For that reason, the phenomenon of competition, as well as the notion of competitiveness cannot be a subject of research and analysis separately from the market, for they are closely connected with all factors, which create and model free-market structures. The way in which competitiveness is seen evolves constantly, especially when reality of economic, political or social life is taken into consideration. In this part of the monograph, the essential concept of companies' competitiveness and its basic dimensions are presented. Moreover, the significance of companies' competitiveness in the specific context of air transportation service sector is outlined.

2.1. The notion and essence of enterprises' competitiveness

Concepts of enterprises' competitiveness

The term 'competitiveness' is quite a complex notion. More and more attention is being paid to it in scientific research. However, it is neither understood nor interpreted unequivocally. One result of research into competitiveness is an array of totally different definitions of the notion in question.[46] Competitiveness of a product, company, branch, sector, economy, or region is defined. The notion of 'competitiveness' can thus be used with respect to companies,

---

[46] The origin of the competitiveness notion in management is customarily looked for in J. Schumpeter's works, who emphasised that there is an on-going race in the capitalist economy and factors found in the company itself are of fundamental significance to the company's development. Nevertheless, development of the 21th century companies is equally contingent on external determinants, i.e. their environment factors.

sectors, regions, nations (countries), and also supranational organisations.[47] In professional literature, an evolution of the notion can be seen, starting with a traditional concept, focusing mainly on the role of tangible assets as competitiveness-determining factors, to a more complex approach, where competitiveness is being determined with a wide variety of factors associated with macro-, meso- and micro- determinants of a company's environment. Therefore, despite the fact that there are many definitions of competitiveness, starting with traditional (cost-based) concepts to more developed (systemic) concepts, it can be assumed that competitiveness is about the ability to compete, in other words, to operate and survive in a competitive surrounding.[48] Competitiveness of a company means that it is capable to compete, or to participate in a market game, relying on skills to compose factors of its competitiveness potential.[49] In its broadest sense, competitiveness was defined by the OECD in the year 1996. According to the OECD, competitiveness is the capacity of companies, sectors, regions, countries and supranational regions to generate a relatively high income of production factors and a relatively high level of employment under conditions of permanently being subjected to international competition.

It is worth emphasising that companies', but also countries' or regions', pursuit of increasing competitiveness is the driving force of all great innovations, and growth in productivity; it stimulates human aspiration and entrepreneurship, and it contributes to the increase of well-being and civilisation growth.[50]

Fundamental aspects of competitiveness

At present, when managing companies, a competitive orientation imperative should be adopted, which means that management systems should be oriented towards multi-dimensional and long-term creation of the company's opportunities in order to obtain/keep its long-term competitive advantage on the market. From the economic perspective of the company's strategy management, three concepts of competitiveness are generally adopted, namely:

---

[47] The category of companies' competitiveness arouses relatively little controversy. Still, problems with the definition occur while evaluating competitiveness of territorial systems, such as a country or a region. Compare, for example, M. Bednarczyk, *Organizacje publiczne. Zarządzanie konkurencyjnością*, Wydawnictwo Naukowe PWN, Kraków 2001; eadem, "Orientacja konkurencyjna w zarządzaniu turystyką" [in:] *Zarządzanie konkurencyjnością biznesu turystycznego w regionach*, ed. M. Bednarczyk, CeDeWu.pl, Warszawa 2011, pp. 13–20.

[48] M. Gorynia, *Luka konkurencyjna na poziomie przedsiębiorstwa a przystąpienie Polski do Unii Europejskiej*, Wydawnictwo Akademii Ekonomicznej w Poznaniu, Poznań 2002, p. 48.

[49] M. Bednarczyk, *Organizacje publiczne...*, op. cit., p. 126 and following.

[50] Eadem, *Otoczenie i przedsiębiorczość w zarządzaniu strategicznym organizacją gospodarczą*, Zeszyty Naukowe Akademii Ekonomicznej w Krakowie, Seria Specjalna: Monografie, Kraków 1996.

- competitive potential,
- competitive advantage,
- competitive position, that is *ex post* competitiveness – resultative (Figure 1).

Figure 1. Dimensions of companies' competitiveness

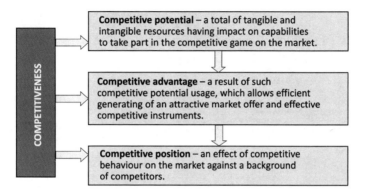

Source: M. Bednarczyk, *Organizacje publiczne. Zarządzanie konkurencyjnością*, Wydawnictwo Naukowe PWN, Warszawa–Kraków 2001, p. 15.

Diagnosing the company's competitiveness requires analysis and evaluation of all three dimensions, which are mutually connected. It is assumed that analysis and evaluation of all dimensions of competitiveness can lead to recognising its source, and thus to creating practical possibilities for its development.[51]

Evaluation of competitive standing can be done in two aspects, namely:

1) static – identification of the company's present competitive situation;
2) dynamic – creating a hypothetical, desired situation of the company's competitive standing in the future.

The analysis of the company's competitive potential is the foundation for evaluating the company's competitive standing. Competitive potential includes tangible and intangible resources, featuring, first and foremost, all key competences that are typical of the company, which distinguish it from its competitors and enable it to gain the competitive advantage that is hard to

---

[51] T. Żabińska, *Klastry turystyczne jako forma współpracy sieciowej i ich rola w budowaniu konkurencyjności regionu* [in:] *Konkurencyjność miast i regionów na globalnym rynku turystycznym*, ed. J. Sala, Polskie Wydawnictwo Ekonomiczne, Warszawa 2010, pp. 734–735.

imitate by its competitors. According to G. Hamel and C. Prahalad, the company's key competences are the key factors to success in its development. They should make the foundation of its strategy concerning competitiveness on the market.[52] Competitive advantage of the company can be achieved as a result of a particular configuration of competitive potential factors, generating an attractive offer on the market and applying efficient competition tools, which allow the company to gain a better competitive standing than that of its competitors.

Tools and methods used to develop the company's competitive strength – its client capital creation of the company's value in particular – are competition tools. Those tools are fundamental to the company's activity in the market:

- they strengthen the vendor's competitive position in relation to competitors (distinguishing the vendor against a background of competitors);
- they neutralise or overcome vendees' negotiation advantage (they lead to gaining acceptance, being favoured by vendees);[53]
- they strengthen negotiation position against other partners of the company when establishing alliances and business networks.

In competitive fight, the company can implement many different competition tools of various structures.[54]

The last dimension of the company's competitiveness is its **competitive position**, which depends largely upon the competitive advantage of the organisation, that is mastering key factors of success (most commonly, the sources of competitive advantage), therefore, it is a synergic sum of its strengths and weaknesses. It is the result of the company's competitive behaviour on the market against a background of competitors. It indicates a position on the scale of economical and extra-economical benefits that the company delivers to its clients compared to the positions that its competitors occupy, according to the same criteria. Basic and synthetic measure of the competitive position

---

[52] G. Hamel, C.K. Prahalad, *Przewaga konkurencyjna jutra. Strategie przejmowania kontroli nad branżą i tworzenia rynków przyszłości*, translation M. Albigowski, Business Press, Warszawa 1999, pp. 213–246.

[53] W. Wrzosek, *Funkcjonowanie rynku*, Polskie Wydawnictwo Ekonomiczne, Warszawa 1994, p. 229.

[54] The efficiency degree of individual tools and the whole competition mechanism can be measured by the vendees' and competitors' speed and depth of response to tools being used, which are the more effective the faster vendees react to them, but the slower the competitors do. But also, it can be measured by the efficiency of networks and inter-organisational business connections created.

of each and every company is its participation in the market and financial standing it obtains.[55]

The role and significance of competitive advantage

At present, in market conditions, the main challenge for a company, as well as an industry, or even a national economy, is developing competence-based and durable competitive advantage. The main purpose of the competitive strategy of each and every company is to gain advantage over the competition, called a 'competitive advantage' or a 'strategic advantage'. The competitive advantage refers to achieving a better result than the rival; generating a higher profit than the industry average; or possessing a major share in the market.

The company's competitiveness depends mainly on its competitive potential. It can thus be assumed that it is closely related to resources or special competences it possesses. However, not all constituents of the company's resources are of the same importance while developing the competitive advantage. Therefore, the main question to be posed in the process of developing the competition strategy concerns the crucial composition of individual components of the potential. The competitive advantage depends not only upon resources' rarity, complicity or non-substitutability, but also upon their adequacy for the rules of the market game. Hence, stability of the competitive advantage is substantial. If the competitor acquires his competence too quickly and introduces innovations more efficiently, his company's hitherto strong competitive position may subside. A short-term competitive advantage on the market results in instability of the company's competitive position and requires a costly reconfiguration of the competitive potential and implementation of different competing tools. In present-day turbulent and constantly changing conditions, stability of the company's competitive advantage is quite illusory.

A classic example is an airline company's entry onto the market in the case of passenger transport of Ryanair or other low-cost airlines. This has dramatically changed sources of competitive advantage of traditional carriers such as the German Lufthansa or the Polish PLL LOT.

An orientated management of companies, especially large companies, should first and foremost include a long-term creation of their ability to compete on the market; on-going proactive monitoring of sources; and ways to acquire and maintain competitive advantage.

---

[55] An attention should be paid to a partial similarity between the competition tools category and competitive position measures, e.g. in both cases, notions of product qualities (features) and costs (prices) appear, however, those notions have quite a different meaning. Source: M. Gorynia, *Luka konkurencyjna na poziomie przedsiębiorstwa...*, op. cit., p. 95.

Perspectives of analysing sources of increase/decrease in the company's competitiveness include both internal and external sources.[56] Internal sources of competitiveness include tangible and intangible assets (competences) of the company,[57] whereas external sources of competitive advantage are found in the environment in which the company operates (the macro-, micro- and meso-environment, meaning regional conditions). In practice, companies search for sources of their competitiveness' increase both inside, and outside, that is, in their surroundings. Various determinants of companies' competitive strength and position can be distinguished.[58]

From many proposed approaches to evaluating the organisation's resources, three main general dimensions can be quoted after J. Fahy, namely[59]:

1. Value – resources should be valuable for the organisation, enabling it to take advantage of the opportunities and neutralise threats that occur in the company's environment.
2. Resistance to imitation and substitution – resources should be characterised by their rarity amongst present, as well as potential competitors, which means that they should be extremely difficult to copy or to substitute with another kind of resources.
3. Appropriation of value – value resulting from the use of resources by the company should be owned by it (this criterion has a special meaning with respect to intangible resources, in relation to which property rights have not been clearly defined).

Looking for competitiveness sources within the company provided the foundation for M.E. Porter's concept of competitive advantage. Thirty years ago, Porter pointed to principles of achieving competitive advantage based on creating added value in all aspects of the company's activity.[60] This concept gained great popularity and continues to be developed in the theory of 'strategic value chains' of the company, region and in supra-regional aspects.

Another approach to looking for sources of competitive advantage is focusing attention on sources found in determinants of the company's external environment. External sources of the company's competitiveness lie in its environment – pertaining to the industry or sector, in which it operates; to regional

---

[56] M. Bednarczyk, *Organizacje publiczne...*, op. cit., p. 15.

[57] Compare discussion on research perspectives, including those resource-oriented and environment-oriented in, e.g.: *Konkurencyjność małych i średnich przedsiębiorstw na polskim rynku turystycznym*, ed. M. Bednarczyk, Wydawnictwo Uniwersytetu Jagiellońskiego, Kraków 2006, pp. 55–72.

[58] Compare e.g. *Konkurencyjność małych i średnich przedsiębiorstw...*, op. cit., pp. 67–68.

[59] Ibid., p. 64.

[60] M.E. Porter, *Competitive Advantage*, Free Press, New York 1985.

or national determinants; or the global ones. Special sets are invented to configure unique resources of the company, necessary from the point of view of the company's efficient adaptation to the environment, called 'fit' (configuration – adjustment). Some global consulting companies have been especially engaged in this field of research. A concept alternative to 'fit' is an integrative approach, founded is the integrative model of the company. Checking the dependencies between the environment and the organisation, and the choice of a defined management strategy focus on the environment analysis in the context of isolated factors, characteristic of the organisation as a whole.[61] A current tendency in the strategic management theory is to look for an effective model of the company's business.[62] The problem of effective configuration of the model, in view of achieving a long-term competitive advantage on the market, is still open and it remains a challenge both to the theory and to practising managers.

For companies, a skilful naming and then maintaining their sources of competitive advantage, and thus eliminating the so-called 'competitive gap', is crucial.[63]

An opinion that significant sources of the company's higher profitability derive not only from a certain position it has within the industry, but rather lie within the company itself and are company specific, is the opinion typical to representatives of the resource-based approach. In the view of this approach, a company's management strategy is seen in a perspective of endogenous increase. From this perspective, sources of the company's potential competitiveness are based upon its ability to learn, change and increase the organisational knowledge. On the other hand, stability of the sources of competitive advantage can be provided through grounding it in the company's distinguishable abilities – innovations characteristic only for that company and developing entrepreneurship within the company with the help of state-of-the-art information technology.[64] American management guru, G. Hamel, and a journalist, B. Breen, in their book titled *The Future of Management*, recognised the

---

[61] Compare M. Bednarczyk, *Otoczenie i przedsiębiorczość w zarządzaniu strategicznym organizacją gospodarczą*, op. cit., pp. 26–27.

[62] Compare B. Nogalski, T. Falencikowski, "Modele biznesów jako nowy obszar badań w naukach o zarządzaniu" [in:] *Nowe obszary badań w naukach o zarządzaniu*, ed. J. Rokita, GWST, Katowice 2015, pp. 80–94.

[63] Gap analysis is one of methods used to investigate adjustment of the already existing strategy and ways the organisation works, to the environment's demands and changes forecasted in the environment in the future. The analysis of the strategy gap is a method of analysis and strategy planning, which aims at determining the level and ways to diminish differences between the organisation's goals and the environment's expectations, with the intention to focus the strategy on analysis and closing the gap. Source: G. Gierszewska, M. Romanowska, *Analiza strategiczna przedsiębiorstwa*, Polskie Wydawnictwo Ekonomiczne, Warszawa 2002, p. 52. Compare M. Gorynia, *Luka konkurencyjna na poziomie przedsiębiorstwa...*, op. cit.

[64] M. Bednarczyk, *Organizacje publiczne...*, op. cit., p. 133.

company's innovation development as a key factor in its future.[65] According to them, current conditions of competition are marked with:[66]

- deregulation and liberalisation of trade which abolish barriers of entering the market, e.g. in air transportation;
- power of the Internet, which did away with the necessity of creating a global infrastructure in order to enter world markets, e.g. Google, eBay;
- spreading fight for customers into the digital space;
- disintegration of the cohesion of large companies through, for example, outsourcing and creating global structures of virtual networks;
- pressure of competitors who have extremely low costs (thanks to their location in India or China).

The companies' competitive reality nowadays is complex and complicated. Therefore, possession of competitiveness potential by a given entity cannot be assumed to be the key factor of success, which guarantees achieving a defined long-term competitive advantage in the extremely turbulent market. Companies have to use all – both internal and external – sources of competitive advantage, so that their competitive position can get stronger or they can maintain their hitherto strong position in the market. Keeping the competitive position on the market does not necessarily imply one-time mastery of specific key factors in a given sector; instead, it is a process of continuous improvement in terms of:

- recognition of opportunities and threats in the environment, those general and industry-specific ones, but also region-specific conditions of functioning;
- creating the ability to compete;
- developing competitive advantage.

There are different and specific determinants in individual sectors, which define the frameworks and forms, as well as the space for strategic competition between companies. The ability to deal with problems associated with competition is particularly important for entities representing air transportation, as this sector is strongly endangered by the impact of global trends and financial crises, and for that reason it is frequently referred to as the 'economic barometer'. Achieving competitive advantage in this particular market is a great challenge especially for airports.

---

[65] G. Hamel G., B. Breen, *The Future of Management*, Harvard Business School Press, Red Horse Ltd., 2008.

[66] Ibid., pp. 71–72.

2.2. Competitiveness in air transportation with a particular focus on the Polish air transport services market

Discussion regarding the role, meaning and shaping of a regional airport competitiveness cannot be held separately from the issue of competition in air transportation or – even more broadly – competitiveness in the whole transportation system, as seen on a regional, national and supranational level (both in an international and global dimension). The phenomenon of competition in transportation, especially in air transportation, can be discussed from many points of view. At this point, significance of air transportation versus other forms of transportation will be considered. Specificity of the air transport services market shall be discussed, moving on to the analysis of competition between individual branches of transport.

Specificity of air transport services market from the perspective of competitiveness

While looking into the issue of competition within the transport services market, we need to consider how the scope of transport services is defined and what its basic features are. Transport services market is determined as 'the area of trading transport services, where potential vendors and vendees make a mutual impact on one another; they create supply and demand, and the equilibrium of prices'[67] and also as 'all of trade and economic relations, including actions of transportation companies (supply) and behaviour of such service clients (demand); but also how organizational structures, which are to facilitate contact of both parties and enable buy-and-sell process, perform.'[68]

Transport services market is influenced by the following features:

- basic market creation mechanisms (such as supply, demand, price);
- entities present within the market (including transport operators, sales agents, airports, financial institutions);
- regulations and mutual connections between the aforementioned elements.

While analysing the issue of how the phenomenon of competition in the transport services market is created, we need to consider what powers affect the market, that is, to investigate the phenomenon of creating needs and

---

[67] W. Grzywacz, *Rynek usług transportowych*, Wydawnictwa Komunikacji i Łączności, Warszawa 1980, p. 29.

[68] *Ekonomika transportu*, ed. J. Burnewicz, Wydawnictwo Uniwersytetu Gdańskiego, Gdańsk 1993, p. 121.

relationships between the demand and the supply.[69] The essence of the market in question is a sequence of individual elements: firstly, there is a need, next a demand (that is, preferences and behaviours of transportation service vendees), in response to which there is a transportation service and then a supply in the transport service market is created; finally, relationships between those elements are established in a form of prices for service being offered (regulations in the transport service market).

Demand and supply are a starting point for the air transportation services market. The need changes into the demand, when there are purchasing funds and information about purchase possibility (service availability). We need to remember that in some part, needs are satisfied within one's own capacity and they are not revealed on the market (e.g. travelling using one's own car).

Thus, primary demand and derived demand need to be distinguished. Primary demand concerns goods and services necessary to satisfy that primary demand directly, whereas derived demand is an effect of a demand for other goods or services. The need, as a result of which there is the demand, is secondary in nature – it is instrumental. The demand for air transportation services is a derived demand, because making an air journey is not a purpose in itself. Although the air journey can be an additional attraction, it is basically treated as a means to fulfilling other needs. As a consequence, the demand for air transportation services depends strongly upon the primary demand for other goods and services, and the fact that it can be fulfilled by substitute services is significant.[70]

Amongst factors impacting the scale of the demand for air transportation, factors of a general nature can be distinguished, such as: income level, gross domestic product, demographic potential (population, age), transport mobility, level of transport fares, quality of service, exchange rates, interest rates, inflation, amount of free time, foreign trade levels, or political situation.

---

[69] The need is a state of the lack of something (a thing, a phenomenon, a process) – it is a factor setting in motion the motivation functions to take action in order to change this state, while the demand equals needs which revealed themselves in the market and have coverage in a purchasing fund.

[70] Definition of substitutability has it that if we move from one point to the other on the same indifference curve, we can increase consumption of one good solely by reducing consumption of a second good. In transport, notions of complementarity and multimodal transport are strongly connected with the notion of substitution. In a complementary approach, transport is seen as a system (a whole), meaning that transportation and economy are one, there is no substitution. In a different approach, air transportation is seen as a branch of transport – there are cases of both complementarity and substitution on the level of separate branches of transportation; for example, car transportation can be substituted with the rail one. The multimodal transport, on the other hand, refers to transportation of goods with the use of at least two different branches of transport. The notion of substitutability among individual branches of transportation is presented further.

The process of purchasing an air service itself consists of 5 stages (Figure 2). All elements in this process influence the final price and willingness to choose the same means of transportation for the second time.

Figure 2. The process of purchasing an air service

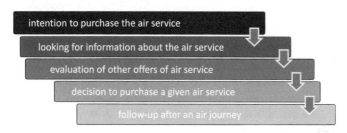

Source: own study.

The demand side is shaped by the supply side, for it responds to the needs of potential entities – first and foremost, the passengers using air transportation and the companies operating within the handling branch. Air transportation is thus characterised by the supply and the demand sides (Figure 3).

Figure 3. Role, significance and functions of air transportation

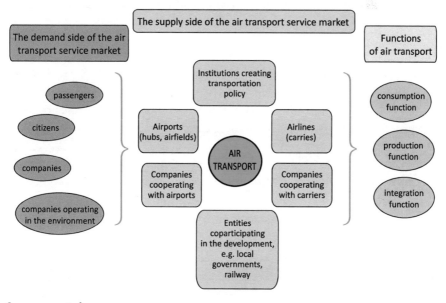

Source: own study.

The notion of demand can be determined as 'a need for service reported on the market in a given time period', whereas the supply of air service is defined as an 'amount of service offered for sale on the market by airline associations in a given time period.'[71] The supply side of air transportation services is created by many entities connected with one another, and the scope of their activity expands depending on changing needs. These are: air transportation companies, including airlines and airline associations; airports – the companies cooperating with operators; and institutions controlling transportation policy.

Transport services are offered by associations (companies and airlines), but also by airports, along with a network of forwarders, travel agencies, tourist agencies, which are complementary in relation thereto. Aviation industry is an element of this system too, providing basic means of operation – i.e. the airplanes for transportation. Special attention should be drawn to the fact, that air transport services market is strongly determined by the specific qualities of the means of transport it uses, i.e. the airplanes.[72] Lack of possibility to balance demand and supply in the global system is a consequence of market-developed differentiation of the industry in question.

As a result of the coexistence of the two sides mentioned previously (the demand and the supply), air transportation fulfils the following functions:

- consumption – satisfying transportation needs with transportation services provided;
- production – creating conditions for business activity, stimulating it and having impact on the market functioning and market exchange;
- integration – consolidation of the country and society via transportation services.

We must keep in mind that air transportation is an activity of cyclic nature. The whole of transportation cycle is called a transportation process, and its nature is a multiphase and multipurpose one. Therefore, air transportation is referred to as an overall, repetitive sequence of actions necessary for transportation of people and cargo.

Meeting transportation needs should maintain interests of both customers and service-providers. No transport organisation (company) can operate

---

[71] *Transport. Problemy transportu w rozszerzonej UE*, eds. W. Rydzykowski, K. Wojewódzki--Król, Wydawnictwo Naukowe PWN, Warszawa 2002, p. 160.

[72] Those are, among others: high cost of the entity purchase (several million USD at least), long service life (about 30 years), high productivity, low cost per unit of the service, low labour consumption of service and transport work performed, high reliability and safety, high standard and requirements in terms of technical support, low environmental risk in relation to different means of transportation.

or have raison d'être, if it does not meet the requirements that characterise the relationship established between transportation service providers and their customers.[73] A dilemma characteristic to air transportation at the turn of the 20th and 21st centuries is a progressing imbalance in the distribution of income between individual entities of the transport market (airports, airlines or entities concerned with the aviation industry[74]). Over the last twenty years – that is, since commencement of the process of complete market facilitation and liberalisation of the transportation market – progressive competition processes are accompanied with a strong focus on the airplanes' production market[75] coupled with strengthening of quasi-monopoly position of the biggest airports.

Activity on the air carriers market is seen as a highly risky one, as rates of return on the investment remain at an extremely low level. What is more, it is often the case that carriers, over a long term, suffer losses, which leads to many instances of bankruptcy, quite frequently recorded in this market. Processes of capital concentration in the air transportation, in a form of mergers and takeovers, intensified under the influence of competition. Companies, which stay behind in the quickly changing reality, suffer a loss, or go bankrupt. These problems particularly concern all European carriers, since

---

[73] For a transportation service manufacturer, it is management efficiency and expanding the scope of transportation, freight forwarding and logistic services, among others. For a customer, it is a situation on the competitive market, quantity and quality of service provided (while following the *just in time* – JIT rule). JIT is a so-called 'on time delivery'. It is a method of production planning and control, based on a rule of elimination from the production process of all losses by manufacturing proper goods in the quantity desired and by the deadline. This leads to such production organisation where all operations are performed exactly at the time they are needed. Taiichi Ohno is believed to be the creator of the *just in time* method. He developed his theory in Toyota plants in the 1950s, based on prerequisites appearing in the Ford system and in the American branch of retail trade. Source: J. Morris, B. Wilkinson, "The Transfer of Japanese Management Techniques to Alien Institutional Environments," *Journal of Management Studies* 32(6), 1995, p. 722, obtained from: http://mfiles.pl/pl/index.php/Just_in_time (access: 2.07.2013).

[74] Aviation industry is a branch, which produces parts for airplanes, gliders, helicopters and aviation fixtures. Main manufacturers in this branch are: in the USA – Boeing (Lockheed Martin – plants in Seattle, Denver, Los Angeles), within the UE – Airbus (main plant in Toulouse), within Russia – Tupolev (Jakovlev, Antonov in Moscow). In Poland the aviation industry was established in the years 1921–1923 and at first, it was manufacturing airplanes on a license. In 1928, Państwowe Zakłady Lotnicze [National Aviation Works] were established. In the years 1960–1990 Polish aviation industry developed production of licensed transportation and farm airplanes. At present, most companies within the industry are owned by foreign investors. The aviation industry from south-eastern Poland is represented by an association called Aviation Valley, which comprises 77 companies employing about 22,000 engineers and technicians.

[75] After mergers and takeovers amongst American manufacturers in the communication airplanes production market, a market structure of duopoly has been created – Boeing in North America and Airbus Industries in Europe.

the degree of their capitalisation is several times lower in comparison with American airlines.[76] This situation is dangerous to all elements of the aviation services market, as lack of stability on the carrier market can become a threat to the functioning of entities representing the aviation equipment production market or the port services market and their derivatives. The growing competition is thus particularly visible in the case of airlines; however, it also concerns airports, which constantly fight to acquire new carriers, ready to offer new connections.[77] For that reason, regulations and contracts between the individual elements of the air transport market are necessary, aimed at regulating such a flow of resources within the whole market, so that their supply ensures its secure functioning. Both airports and other entities of the aviation market should receive sufficient inflows of cash. Those entities are seen as attractive places to allocate investment funds and aviation industry is additionally supplied with financial means from military orders. Airports are supplied with subsidies from central, regional, or local governments.

There is a subtle balance between all elements of the system, as supply of financial means takes place mainly via one of its elements – the carrier market. Both airports and the whole aviation industry can achieve income only indirectly via efficient functioning of the air transportation market. This fact is one of the determinants of change happening now, and of the specificity of the current air transportation market.

Substitute competition

Competitiveness of a regional airport is dependent on access to substitute services in terms of transportation. Transport consists of several branches; one can use road, rail, water, or air transportation service. A potential passenger makes the choice of the most appropriate means of transportation, thus a process called substitute competition[78] takes place between individual branches of transport.

---

[76] According to a study conducted by market analysts, in Europe, only 3 or 4 mega-carriers will remain, among which the ones most frequently mentioned are British Airways, Lufthansa, SAS and Air France, supported by smaller airlines associated with them. Such a tendency can support processes of deregulation and liberalisation of the branch because governments, in view of capital concentration, will not be willing to grant subsidies, using taxpayers money, to national carriers owned by a foreign capital.

[77] Urząd Lotnictwa Cywilnego, Departament Rynku Transportu Lotniczego, *Analiza rynku transportu lotniczego w Polsce w latach 2004–2006*, Warszawa 2008, obtained from: http://www.ulc.gov.pl/_download/wiadomosci/ 09_2008/analiza1.pdf (access: 10.05.2013).

[78] The core of this process is the phenomenon of non-substitutability in transportation resulting from homogeneity of transportation services with respect to economy; this enables mutual substitution of one means of transportation with another, carrying analogous cargo or

The following factors decide, among others, about the passenger's choice of a means of transportation: financial means possessed, time constraints, capability to provide convenience and comfort of journey, distance from the desired destination. These factors have impact on the potential passenger's decision to choose the right form of transportation over the alternatives. The demand for transportation service is characterised by non-substitutability of services that have in common a high elasticity of demand.

Such competition is mainly about rivalry for a potential client; propagation and facilitation of access to services offered; and efforts to provide an even cheaper transportation service, but at the same time, of higher quality.

A detailed comparative analysis of both advantages and disadvantages of the four main branches of transportation: road (bus/coach), rail, water, and air, is presented in Table 6.

Functioning of the air transport market is determined by its characteristic features, among which the most important are: simultaneity of the production and the consumption of the air transportation service; strong variation of service in time; misalignment of transport flows in the opposite direction; low resilience of transportation service demand; international character of service; tightly regulated legal forms of carriers; multiple companies operating in aviation traffic service directly or indirectly; cargo and courier mail, usually of higher quality. Those qualities strongly determine the demand for the aviation service offered. It is assumed that air transportation is more advantageous for a potential passenger in case of long-distance journeys, in particular transcontinental ones. For shorter distances, especially when high-speed trains are an available alternative, the choice of an airplane as a means of transportation can be debatable.

The competition between the different kinds of transportation listed above is also about rivalry for investments, and for friendly policies in the given country, such as advantageous tax policy or regional development policy. In many countries, air transportation stands in an unfavourable position in the competition against railways and road transportation, or inland navigation. The other branches of transportation mentioned are subsidised heavily. Numerous and substantial investments on a large scale are being made, especially roads and railway infrastructure is heavily subsidised, indirectly also via a suitable tax policy (including tax exemptions for fuels).

---

loads of passengers on similar distances. Source: K. Bentkowska-Senator, Z. Kordel, *Transport w turystyce*, Wydawnictwo Uczelniane WSG, Bydgoszcz 2008, p. 22.

Table 6. Advantages and disadvantages of particular branches of transportation

RAIL TRANSPORTATION

Advantages:
- lower cost of tickets in comparison to air travel
- relatively high level of journey safety
- possibility to rest and sleep at night
- in the so called *high speed trains*: relatively high comfort of journey, high speed and high level of safety

Disadvantages:
- limitations resulting from timetables
- necessity to use additional transportation for transfers
- relatively low comfort of journey
- relatively low travelling speed
- necessity of carrying the luggage while transferring
- risk of crime (especially thefts)

COACH/BUS TRANSPORTATION

Advantages:
- one of the cheapest forms of transportation per participant
- possibility of getting directly to a destination (a tourist attraction, accommodation)
- possibility of discovering a passing by scenery
- luggage loaded in a departure place, no risk of losing the luggage

Disadvantages:
- lengthening time of journey
- limitations in the size of luggage
- necessity of crossing many border crossings (slowly being eliminated by international regulations)
- risk of collisions, road accidents (the highest rate as compared to other means of transport)

AIR TRANSPORTATION

Advantages:

- comfort of travelling
- high level of safety, the lowest rate of accident risk
- comfort of travelling above 2,000 km
- the only means of transport, apart from water transport, to be used for intercontinental journeys
- short time of travel and high speed of travelling (taking time of reaching transportation points and time for transfers into consideration)
- possibility to use connections of the *point-to-point* type (directness of connections, no necessity to transfer)
- reliability, high volume, and high frequency of transfers
- possibility of tickets purchase at a relatively fair price
- high safety level and travel comfort

Disadvantages:

- relatively high cost (i.e. a relatively high ticket price but thanks to LCC it is possible to choose one of the cheapest options of getting to desired destinations)
- high terrorism risk
- limitations in journey planning resulting from flight schedules and airport's location (limited areal availability due to airport's location and thus a burdensome necessity of getting to the airport, which is not always in the traveller's place of residence)
- change of flight times that causes additional costs and depends on the possibility to change the reservation
- restrictions or possible delays due to weather conditions
- necessity to use additional transport for transfers

WATER TRANSPORTATION

Advantages:

- low price (as compared to flight tickets)
- possibility to order meals
- high comfort of journey
- when organizing certain types of journey it is the only means of transportation, apart from air travel (getting to islands)
- possibility of additional attractions, getting to know some extra places

Disadvantages:

- low speed of travel, the journey lengthens greatly
- limitations resulting from timetables
- restrictions or possible delays due to weather conditions
- necessity to use additional transport for transfers
- many potential passengers forgo this form of transportation due to seasickness or fears and anxieties

Source: own study based on *Entrepreneurship in Tourism and Sport Business*, ed. M. Bednarczyk, Fundacja dla Uniwersytetu Jagiellońskiego, Kraków 2008, p. 94 (drawings by Joanna Olesiak).

Having said that, it is assumed that intermodal competition should be a political goal of air transportation.[79] It would allow the determination of opportunities for aviation service providers – it would show deficiencies existing in innovation and efficiency, with indication of shortages in relation to competitors on the side of other transportation branches (road, water or rail).

Competition increase in the sector depends not only on vendees, but also on competitive powers and changes taking place in the relationships between them, which imply evolution of the sector.[80] As the sector moves through the next stage of its life cycle, the importance and competition powers change, which in transportation is still compounded by diversity. Among many factors specific to individual markets or relations there are: cultural and ethnic bonds, competitors' activity, availability of alternative means of transportation, tourism attractiveness, costs of transportation service, and flow of manpower. From the perspective of the Polish regional airports development, air transportation competitiveness in a global and national aspect, as well as the perspective of the European region, are all very significant, therefore, those issues are to be discussed further in this monograph.

The functioning of Polish airports from the perspective of domestic and European air transportation market competition

Airports need to be seen in the context of how the whole Polish transportation system functions, and also in the aspect of the EU transportation policy. It is believed that relevant political-legal, investment and financial frameworks should be created for proper development of the transportation market. Therefore, the notion of competitiveness of the air transportation sector remains within the sphere of competence of the national governments in individual countries, as well as EU authorities and bodies.

The EU policy should not be aimed at imposing excessive loads on services within the EU, for it would not be favourable for increasing competitive advantage of European airports compared to other ports. The tendency should be to improve efficiency of air traffic management, and the EU aviation industry should become a pioneer in using low-carbon fuels.[81] The air transportation sector is, in its nature, global, and therefore actions to increase airports' flow capacity should be optimised, in order to meet the increasing

---

[79] For intermodal framework of competition in transportation policy, see A. Eisenkopf, "Der intermodale Wettbewerbsrahmen der Verkehrspolitik," *Internationales Verkehrswesen* 3, 2005, pp. 71–76.

[80] Compare M.E. Porter, *Strategia konkurencji*, translation A. Ehrlich, Polskie Wydawnictwo Ekonomiczne, Warszawa 1992, p. 165.

[81] *White Paper: Roadmap to a Single European Transport Area – Towards a competitive and resource efficient transport system*, Brussels 2011, 28 March 2011 COM/2011/0144/final, p. 8.

demand for travel to (and from) third countries, but also to those areas of Europe, which are less well connected.[82] In aviation, all those actions will lead to gaining competitive advantage, which in turn will grant the EU the position of a 'global airport'. Among the biggest threats to the development of the European aviation are the forecasts connected with constraints on the flow capacity of big European airports. For Polish airports, this is a tremendous development opportunity.

The notion of correlation between air transportation competitiveness and the country's competitiveness should also be taken into consideration. Air transportation has a substantial impact on how competitiveness of the whole national economy is developing, but at the same time, its status and development are a derivative of the economic development. By contrast, emerging of individual countries' competitiveness has a high significance for different branches of the economy, including transportation. In the rankings of individual countries' economic competitiveness, the degree of transport development in a given country is one of the major criteria for evaluation.

Table 7 presents SWOT analysis of transport in Poland. This analysis, being an integral part of the diagnosis of Polish transport, is presented in two aspects: national and EU.[83]

In a synthetic manner, the above analysis points to strengths of Polish transport, which can contribute to increasing opportunities and avoiding development threats, if used correctly. This compilation leads to an important assertion: location of Poland in the centre of Europe, at the crossing of main communication tracts, and favourable topographic determinants of our country's territory, create extremely favourable conditions for transit traffic services, as well as for development of companies operating in transportation, freight forwarding and logistics areas. In order to use those advantages fully, it is necessary to develop and modernise the already existing transportation infrastructure, among other things. This infrastructure, if adequately equipped with modern technological solutions, should not only improve the quality of citizens' lives, but also strengthen the competitive position of Polish economy in international markets.[84]

---

[82] By 2050 those actions can result in a more than a double increase in the aviation activity within the EU, whereas in other cases, the so-called high-speed railway should provide transportation on average distances.

[83] In the table presented there are no criteria or their weights in terms of weaknesses and strengths, as well as opportunities and threats on the infrastructure and market transportation level, as a result of which its content can serve a demonstrative purpose only.

[84] *Strategia Rozwoju Transportu do 2020 roku (z perspektywą do 2030 roku)*, Ministerstwo Transportu, Budownictwa i Gospodarki Morskiej, Warszawa, dated 22 January 2013, http://www.transport.gov.pl/files/0/1795904/130122SRTnaRM.pdf. Ministerstwo Infrastruktury, *Strategia Rozwoju Transportu do 2020 roku (z perspektywą do 2030 roku). Główne kierunki w zakresie lotnictwa (projekt)*, Warszawa 2011, pp. 19–21.

Table 7. SWOT analysis of Polish transport

Strengths	Weaknesses
Infrastructure • relatively large supply and potential of existing networks, ports, terminals and nodes; • already existing conditions for development of a full variety of branch and technical forms of infrastructure; • good topographical conditions of the country (flat area and no seismic activity), favourable for building straight routes (important for high speed systems and others with a high standard guaranteed); • relatively small population density outside urban areas; • layout of inland water routes, beneficial from the transport needs point of view; • costs of environmental impact of transportation included in external costs; • low level of urbanisation and industrialisation in many areas, facilitating development of transportation infrastructure; • implementation of a 'user pays for infrastructure system' principle, including national roads; • introduction of ETC system. **Transportation markets** • high number of core and auxiliary companies in overland transportation; • dynamic development of TSL companies; • high number of employees, and well qualified staff in the majority of companies; • numerous and modern fleet of truck vehicles; • skilful and effective car companies management, conditions and possibilities to reduce their costs.	**Infrastructure** • high degree of wear of many line and point infrastructure elements; • occurrence of bottlenecks and missing links in the network; • local network layout and availability is uneven; • lack of network adjusted for high speed railway traffic; • lack of coherent network of motorways and dual carriageways; • financing of the national roads infrastructure with liabilities – the escalating KFD [national road fund] debt; • lack of continuity in terms of technical class of connections between agglomerations; • poor inter-modality; • weakness of modules integrating different types of networks; • poor utilization of inland water transportation due to insufficient adjustment of water routes to navigable conditions; • nuisance of many transport network elements to citizens and the natural environment; • few features of intelligent and innovative networks; • still ineffective and costly solutions in terms of preventing negative impact on the environment; • progressive deterioration in quality of railways sections; • low effectiveness of railway infrastructure management by the governing body. **Transportation markets** • transportation demand bias, directed to road transport mainly; • out-dated means of rail and water transportation; • low competitive position of air and sea carriers on the market; • low relevance of cargo air transport;

- poor quality of rail and bus/coach passenger transport;
- weak financial standing of the transportation and logistics sector and a high rate of unprofitable companies;
- large number of accidents, especially road traffic, but also at level crossings; high environmental burden, especially from motor transportation;
- low aviation mobility of the society;
- administrative-legal barriers limiting the capability of Polish harbours to handle highly-processed goods;
- low competitiveness of the railway sector in goods transport, resulting from high costs of operation and poor quality of infrastructure.

Opportunities	Threats
Infrastructure	**Infrastructure**

Opportunities

Infrastructure
- creating a network of connections in the neighbouring countries adjoining the Polish transportation network – increasing international availability of transportation;
- possibility to receive EU co-financing for infrastructure projects in the new 2014–2020 financial perspective;
- social support for activities connected with building new road infrastructure (modernisation of structure (dual carriageways) and railway infrastructure (modernisation of the present network and building high standard lines);
- achieving inter-branch integration and European interoperability of the network – elimination of missing links in the local and regional network;
- social support for building ring roads for towns and cities located within networks of international and national importance;
- development of innovative IT technologies, supporting traffic management and safety, and integrating different transportation branches in order to use the existing resources more efficiently;
- complementing traditional networks with intelligent and innovative transport networks;

Threats

Infrastructure
- maintenance of existing barriers, delaying implementation of the infrastructure modernisation;
- climate changes and growing risk of natural disasters occurrence;
- instability of networks modernisation effects caused by its premature devastation;
- increased costs of transport impact on the natural environment share of external costs;
- creating new and competitive infrastructure in neighbouring countries;
- relatively large share of environmentally-valuable areas in the country area – high risk of environmental-spatial conflicts, social protests, delaying and making implementation of infrastructure projects difficult;
- prolonged economic crisis in Europe and thus reduction of co-financing for infrastructure projects implementation from the EU budget, as well as private investors.

Opportunities	Threats
• emergence of new sources and mechanisms (warranties, insurance, limiting hazards) for supporting infrastructure financing; • EU transportation policy supporting the development of inland water transportation; location on a crossing of European transport corridors. **Transportation markets** • opportunities to maintain and strengthen the demand for Polish road transport services in the European market; • existence of a large and stable demand for transport being the foundation of stable functioning of transport, freight forwarding and logistics companies; • internalisation of the external costs of transportation, as a factor for rationalising the development of the transportation sector; • good demand and technological conditions for high-speed railway development; • increasing interest on the part of the users in good quality mass transportation; • increasing effectiveness of means used in systems to improve transportation safety; • strong inter-branch and technological integration of the transportation system; • inflow of foreign capital, intensifying potential and updating of Polish transport; • geographical location enabling development of passenger and cargo air connections in the east - west direction; • opportunity to increase the quality of service provided by the transportation and logistics sector as a result of improved conditions for competition development in that market.	**Transportation markets** • insufficient funds for the modernisation of transport and logistic systems; • marginalisation or displacement of some large Polish carriers and operators from the market; • ineffectiveness of means to reduce environmental impact of transportation; • maintaining strong dynamics of individual motorisation development; • intensification of competition in transportation markets; • progressing impairment of the transit role played by the Polish transportation system; • impact of the external costs internalisation on the level of road carriers' competitiveness; • growing trend of oil, raw materials and energy prices in the world markets; disintegration of regional and supra-regional railway transport systems.

Source: based on *Strategia Rozwoju Transportu do 2020 roku (z perspektywą do 2030 roku)*, Ministerstwo Transportu, Budownictwa i Gospodarki Morskiej, Warszawa, dated 22 January 2013, http://www.transport.gov.pl/files/0/1795904/130122SRTnaRM.pdf, pp. 31–32 (access: 10.09.2013).

Shaping the competitive position of a given regional airport within Poland is determined by the status of the whole Polish economy. It is a derivative of the Polish transportation sector development, aviation in particular, and also of its native region's importance. From the point of view of the regional airport, it is not only the competitive position of a given country that plays an important role. Competitiveness of the given airport's native region is crucial as well, which shall be discussed in the next section.

3. FOUNDATIONS FOR ASSESSING COMPETITIVENESS
OF AN AIRPORT

In the ever more competitive world of air transportation, maintaining a competitive position of individual airports in the air transport market is increasing in importance. Ensuring the current and future competitive strength is a serious challenge to all airports, but especially to regional airports, because their position – in comparison with the so-called big ports (hubs) – is not as stable and unthreatened. This chapter discusses the key elements for the analysis and evaluation of airport competitiveness. An overview of methods and tools used in competitiveness evaluation is shown, leading to the selection of features, which have significant impact on a competitive position of an airport.[85]

3.1. Fundamental aspects of airport competitiveness

The dynamic development of the market for air transport services, coupled with the processes of liberalization and deregulation, have led to increased competition between individual airports.[86] It turns out that the marketing approach, which assumes airport's monopoly on the service, is out-dated. In recent years, airport areas in many regions have been significantly expanded. This has been largely influenced by the emergence of the so-called low-cost

---

[85] The presented analysis and assessment takes into account, among others, the traditionally understood 'airport environment' as the external source of its competitiveness. The study did not cover the communication environment of the ports in the strict sense, since the test procedure would require separate research methods and techniques that would go beyond the adopted model. The term 'external communication environment' means the outer informational space of the company, defining the competitive factors of the company in an information network, as a new dimension of its environment. M. Bednarczyk, "Wpływ otoczenia komunikacyjnego na redefinicje strategii konkurencji polskich przedsiębiorstw" [in:] *Konkurencyjność przedsiębiorstw wobec wyzwań XXI wieku*, Wydawnictwo Akademii Ekonomicznej, Wrocław 1999, pp. 239–243.

[86] Cf. P.D. Barrett, "Airport competition in the deregulated European aviation market," *Journal of Air Transport Management* 6, 2000, pp. 13–27.

airlines. Passengers, who can purchase an airline ticket at a favourable price, are willing to devote more time to getting to the airport, which offers them that opportunity. The development of transport infrastructure also has a major impact on airport competitiveness. Airports have to compete against each other for customers.[87]

The growth in air traffic volume requires airports to increase their infrastructure spending. They need to improve the efficiency of runways, the assignment of slots and ground operations. This is associated with the need to work with new and still very expensive technological solutions. The processes of deregulation and liberalization of the airports, which have been taking place around the world for the last several years, led to airports becoming prone to fierce competition. On the other hand, the quality of airport service is affected by separate regulations (e.g. such concerning safety or protection of the environment). Until a few decades ago, most airports were state owned. The gradual privatization carried out today in many countries is causing an increase in shareholders' expectations for profit and quality management. The state authorities' interest concerns the influence of airport operations on the attractiveness of a given area. Another strategically important issue for local authorities is to examine the impact of the airport on the area, depending on the fact whether it is a central or a regional airport. In the end, the important issue is the question of efficiency of central and regional airports as well as their capacity, which will open new development opportunities (e.g. the creation of new jobs).

Another new indication of increased competition should be noted at this point, associated with the expansion of low-cost carriers' offer throughout Europe. The development of 'new' airports is happening: the secondary ports, which compete with the 'old' (primary) airports. This process generally concerns ports serving large urban agglomerations.[88] Developing the 'new' ports involves a better adaptation of their offer to the requirements of low-cost carriers, and the fact that large ('old') airports have reached or are about to reach their maximum capacity.[89] The 'new' ports are mainly former military airbases, adapted to the needs of civil aviation and often burdened at the initial stage of their operation with serious problems and threat of liquidation.

---

[87] The question of the importance of competition for the activity of the airport is considered also in terms of competitiveness between the airport terminals – cf. P. McLay, A. Reynolds-Feighan, "Competition between Airport terminals: The Issues Facing Dublin Airport," *Transportation Research: Part A* 40, 2006, pp. 181–203.

[88] These 'new' ports are often situated far away from the main agglomerations. However, they claim the right to use their name.

[89] Its elements are lower airport charges, the short time between landing and the next start, the basic level of service at the passenger station without unnecessary – additional services (i.e. not essential according to the business philosophy of low-cost carriers).

In Poland, it is also possible that such airports will emerge, but this would involve considerable investment costs.

The success or failure of a given airport consists of circumstances stemming from many different planes of interaction, both external and internal. Such issues as contracts or acts of environmental law passed, strikes, disasters, various events taking place even far from the airports in question (e.g. the earthquake and tsunami in Japan, unexpected political instability – e.g. in 2011 in the Middle East and North Africa), as well as various seemingly insignificant events (for example the recent fad to release paper sky lanterns, balloons and other such objects[90]) all influence the position of a regional airport. The fundamental question is whether and how much do these factors ultimately affect the competitive standing of a given airport, a Polish regional airport in particular.

Analysing competitiveness of an airport is not an easy task, as it requires extensive research area. In assessing the competitive position, not only internal factors should be taken into account but also changes in the environment of the organization, as they have a decisive impact on the stability of the competitive position, which in turn depends on the stability of its market advantage in a changing environment. The company draws up resources from the outside, providing products and/or services in return, which are necessary to other organizations or particular individuals. It is believed that the success of a company has its origins in the fastest and most accurate diagnosis of its business environment.[91]

In terms of its structure, and the way it impacts the organization (directly or indirectly), it is customary to make a distinction between objective and subjective environment.

The **subjective environment** includes stakeholders, the so called 'interest groups' or impact groups, organization's supporters, shareholders or partners, who largely determine the behaviour of the given company or public

---

[90] The fad to release heated balloons raises safety concerns among airport workers, as lanterns fall on runways and fuel base. The problem increasingly affects also Polish airports, e.g. WAW or GDN. Source: http://warszawa. gazeta.pl/warszawa/1,34889,9062660,Lampiony_ zmora_lotniska__Spadaja_na_pasy_startowe.html (access: 20.06.2014). Drones pose another current threat to the safe functioning of an airport.

[91] The organization's environment is made up of what does not belong to it, has a space and time dimension; has or may have influence on the organization or may be influenced by it in the future. Such general definition of institution's environment includes both the impact of general and variable economic conditions on the competitiveness of organizations, social infrastructure, competition policy; as well as the opposite – the impact of institutions (especially big and strategic institutions) on the economy of the country, their organization, changes in government policy and legal regulations. Source: M. Bednarczyk, *Organizacje publiczne. Zarządzanie konkurencyjnością*, Wydawnictwo Naukowe PWN, Warszawa–Kraków 2001, p. 68.

organization in the market.[92] In the case of an airport, we can subdivide them into a number of entities that are economically linked thereto, and therefore, keenly interested in the development of that airport. These are mainly: airlines, representatives of the tourism industry (tour operators, restaurateurs, hoteliers etc.), representatives of the region (regional authorities, local governments of the lower level), entities responsible for the promotion and development of the region, and central government authorities.[93]

Market competition requires thinking about it in terms of a strategic triangle – the company, the customers, and the rivals. However, in the case of an airport, the competition is better presented in the form of a polygon (Figure 4) including the following groups of entities:

- competitive entities – rivals and competitors. These are, above all else, airports, airfields, as well as service providers offering services substitutable for these provided by airports, i.e. entities representing rail or road transport;
- current and potential clients – airlines, but also passengers; this group may expand over time due to specific conditions;
- partners – i.e. authorities of the city or the region;
- other entities which are interested in the development of the airport;
- supervising entities and entities having influence on the situation of the airport – acting in supervisory capacity, but also those responsible for regulation and enforcement of transport policy in relation to airports.

These entities operate on different levels, and they have varying influence on the development of the airport. Conditions of shaping the development of the airport in question are determined by numerous factors, both those directly concerning the port itself (factors present in the examined area), and factors occurring outside the registry of a given airport. It is assumed that the environment includes all the elements outside the influence of the company or only minimally influenced by it; all those elements, which the company must identify, analyse, anticipate, and assess the potential impact of those factors on the decisions it makes. All of these factors, by their very existence and specificity (type, nature) affect the development of the competitive position of an airport.

---

[92] Ibid., p. 73.

[93] Airports provide infrastructure and ground services whilst airlines provide the transport service itself. Air traffic control is responsible for security, and State authorities establish the regulatory and legal framework. Source: B. Liberadzki, L. Mindura, *Uwarunkowania rozwoju systemu transportowego Polski*, Wydawnictwo Instytutu Technologii Eksploatacji – PIB, Warszawa–Radom 2007, p. 37.

Figure 4. Subjective environment (stakeholders) constituting the competitive framework of an airport

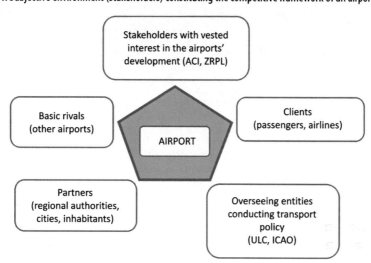

Source: own study.

The **objective environment** can be divided according to its proximity to the company – i.e. 'closer' and 'further' – and the typical classification distinguishes macro-, meso- and micro-environment (often referred to as 'competitive environment').[94]

The competitive environment includes all economic entities that have a cooperative relationship with the company or compete against it. The most important components of the competitive environment include suppliers, buyers, and existing as well as potential competitors.[95] A feature of the competitive environment is that there is feedback between its members and the company: competitors in the competitive environment directly affect the company, but the company has the opportunity to actively influence the environmental stimuli. Mutual relations have the features of an economic game and may not only be studied and anticipated, but also actively influenced by the company through its management.

---

[94] Competitiveness can be associated with different levels of economic system. In economics, we distinguish six main levels of hierarchy of economic systems: micro-micro, micro, meso, macro, regional (in relation to a group of countries), and global. Micro-micro level is the lowest, and it concerns individual consumers, individual entrepreneurs and individual employees. This is the basic level of analysis in economics. The analysis units here are the economic aspects of human behaviour. Micro level includes businesses (except for one-man businesses) and households consisting of more than one consumer. Source: *Kompendium wiedzy o konkurencyjności*, eds. M. Gorynia, E. Łaźniewska, Wydawnictwo Naukowe PWN, Warszawa 2010, p. 51.

[95] G. Gierszewska, M. Romanowska, *Analiza strategiczna przedsiębiorstwa...*, op. cit., p. 31.

The analysis of the competitive environment consists of situating the company among its competitors and studying its position, as well as strength and attractiveness of the sector in which it operates. It also helps to determine the strategic group of businesses, i.e. companies with similar ideas when it comes to competition, in order to identify areas of possible strategic agreements with other players.[96] This is the basis for creating business strategies to compete in the market, as the primary segment of the business environment is the sector in which it competes. Airports are an essential part of the transport system, which is why the issue of their functioning should be examined from the specific perspective of air transport industry.

Transport, including air transport, meets the basic needs of the population, providing services to material production and non-production operations, which is a prerequisite for the existence of commodity market and the market economy, as well as for any mass production. It enables social division of labour, that is, cooperation and specialization of material production; it stimulates growth of international trade in goods and international specialization of labour; it integrates economic, cultural and political activities; it is an important factor in the localization of production and human settlement; it has a significant impact on increasing the mobility of the population and the development of tourism; it is an important contributor to gross national product; and so forth.[97] All these spheres intermingle and by entering into mutual interactions, they stimulate each other. These factors can account for the success or failure of the airport, thus they are important determinants or inhibitors. Therefore, the issues of the functioning of the transport market were adopted as a starting point for further analysis and, in turn, as a benchmark.

Various factors decide about the development and the shaping of holistically understood transport system – air transport included – and they can be systematized in order to single out appropriate sets of factors, e.g. demographic, economic, technological or political.

An important element in the analysis of an airport's functioning is the observation of the processes and changes from the point of view of different interest groups, in the meso-environment and the competitive environment. We are dealing with factor-driven competitiveness (competitive ability), which depends on tangible and intangible resources available to the airport,

---

[96] M. Bednarczyk, *Otoczenie i przedsiębiorczość w zarządzaniu strategicznym organizacją gospodarczą*, Wydawnictwo Akademii Ekonomicznej, Kraków 1996, pp. 29–30.

[97] The issue of the impact of air transport on the economy of the region, especially on the development of tourism and tourist traffic and the operation of tourist services is subjected to detailed analyses, e.g. A. Kowalczyk, *Relacje zachodzące między rozwojem transportu lotniczego a rozwojem turystyki* [in:] *Współczesne uwarunkowania i problemy rozwoju turystyki*, Jagiellonian University, Institute of Geography and Spatial Management, Kraków 2013.

and on the changing conditions in the surrounding environment.[98] These factors belong to different areas of external conditions: macro (political and legal factors, economic, technological, etc.), meso (among others, these are factors related to the region, the industry, the co-operation of the airport with other entities), micro (i.e. the competitive area in the narrow sense) and internal (activities carried out by the authorities of the port itself, for instance in terms of creation and development of safety, quality, marketing, and other policies).

All circumstances from the interest perspective of an airport, which represents transportation industry, should be taken into consideration. It is believed that the sector (the industry)[99] to which a given company belongs has an extremely significant impact on creating opportunities and threats for that company, especially at macro level.

It is possible to specify a group of inherent factors in the market environment, which are relevant for all companies, to a greater or lesser extent. These include, among others, state fiscal policies, mechanisms and regulations on freedom of establishment, the level of economic growth, economic trends, availability and interest rates on loans, the demand and supply of skilled labour, and labour regulations. All of these factors can be singled out and then systematized, keeping in mind that we should look at them from the point of view of airports' interests, as well as from the perspective of the entire transport system, especially air transport.

Political-legal factors, but also factors resulting from the historical perspective – due to historical reasons – are strongly linked and have a huge impact on creating opportunities and threats for companies such as airports. Particularly noteworthy here are geopolitical factors, because the situation of airports should be considered from the perspective of changes taking place at the international level. One of the most significant trends for air transport in the world is the 'deregulation trend' (elimination of prohibitions, restrictions, legal barriers, customs etc.). With these transformations, the conditions of competition in the world markets are changing; international competition in the aviation market evolves and becomes more and more fierce. Undoubtedly, the economic world and the political world are now becoming more intertwined, and their relationship is not always beneficial for companies.

---

[98] The objective inevitability of changes in the environment, organisation and the connecting structures between them is characteristic. Both the organization and its environment are constantly changing. According to the opinion of P. Drucker the only constant in the organization is change.

[99] For example, government policy strongly differentiates the conditions for enterprises, depending on whether or not they belong to preferred sectors (industries). Priority sectors for the economy enjoy preferential loans, government procurement, protective custom tariffs as well as other systemic and financial advantages.

Another important group of factors concerning airport environment is a set of economic factors, which – considered from the perspective of a given country – we refer to as macro-economic factors. These include economic values affecting all entities and processes in the economy of the country concerned. They are, without a doubt, strongly related to political factors. From these two areas, the political-legal and the economic, very important interdependencies derive, which are decisive when it comes to financing opportunities for airports. Tourism is a particularly important industry for the air transport sector – there is constant feedback occurring between tourism and air travel. It is therefore necessary to describe the main factors affecting the development of tourism and try to analyse the mechanisms and regulations taking place between these two branches of the economy.

Air transport, including the activity of an airport, is also strongly dependent on technological development, as well as progressing development in information technology etc. Progress in the field of new technologies has a huge impact on services provided by air transport, especially on improving the quality and safety of the services, issues of passenger check-ins, facilities, and so forth, promoting and making transport services available on a mass scale. Demographic and socio-cultural considerations are also linked to the above issue.

Trends are being shaped as a result of globalization, liberalization and deregulation processes, as well as major cultural and sports events (e.g. the EURO 2012), which are linked to political and legal factors. This shows that all these factors interact with each other, which in turn determines the functioning of airports.

It should be emphasized that the success of an airport depends on the conditions that form around it: the point in the infrastructure of air transport system. Thus, for the discussed factors, an attempt was made to classify, systematize and illustrate the position of the airport in relation to all the aforementioned core segments and groups of factors affecting its operation (Figure 5).

Determinants on the macro level constitute the background and the plane for further consideration, which aims at demonstrating opportunities and risks for the whole airport system. Such issues will become focus of attention as political-legal and geopolitical conditions, activities by entities at international level, the policy of the central government and on supranational level; as well as economic, environmental, technological and security-related factors on a global scale. Therefore, the macro-environment can be subdivided into the following segments: economic environment, technological environment, social environment, demographic environment, political and legal environment, and international environment.[100] It is generally assumed that

---

[100] G. Gierszewska, M. Romanowska, *Analiza strategiczna przedsiębiorstwa*, Polskie Wydawnictwo Ekonomiczne, Warszawa 2002, p. 35. M. Bednarczyk singled out also the environ-

Figure 5. Airport and its impact spheres

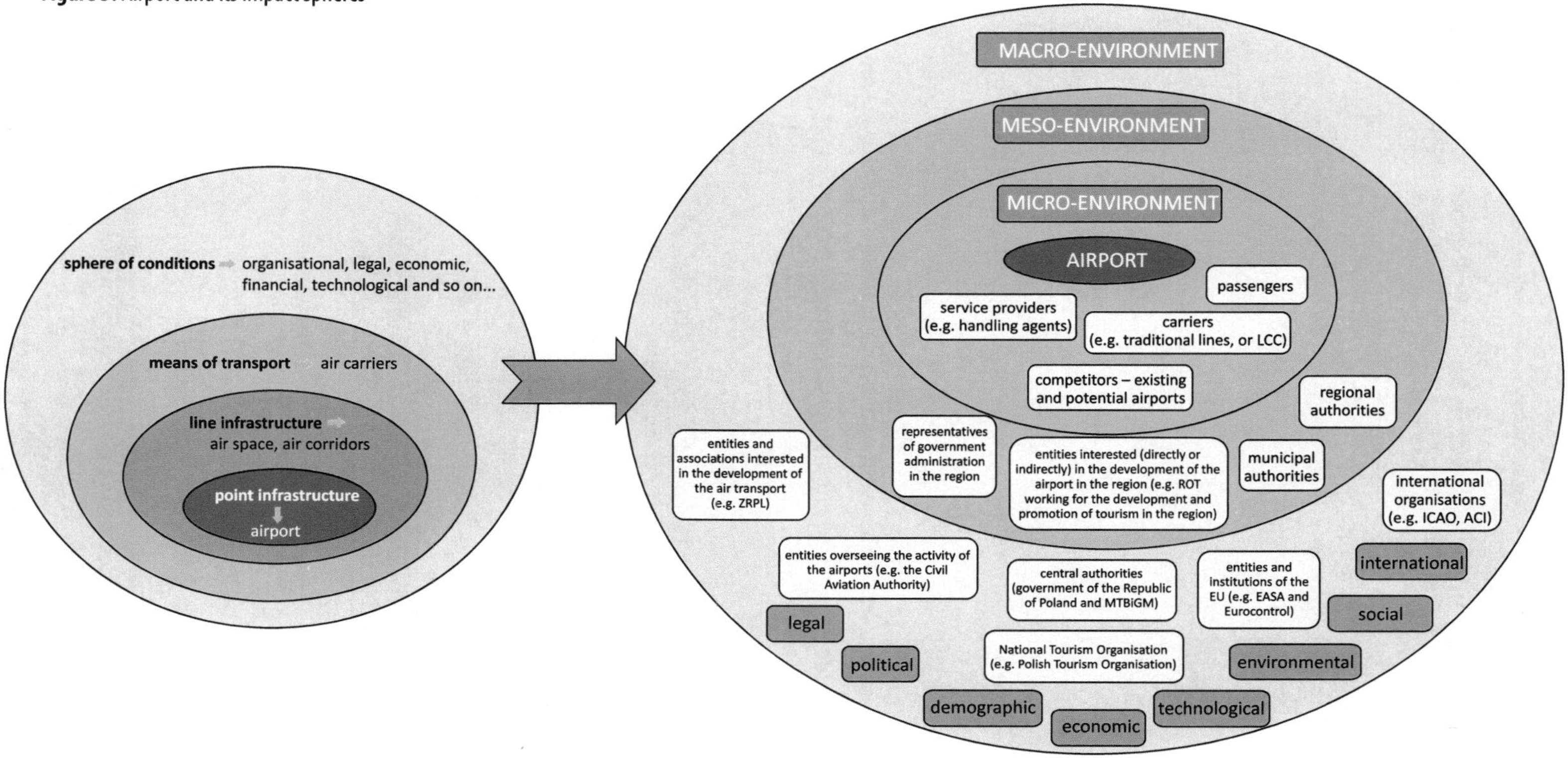

Source: own study.

the segmentation of the macro-environment involves its division into typical segments, which are interconnected, and thus jointly influence the choice of a competitive strategy for the given airport.

Meso-environment is the regional environment, and it determines the conditions within the administrative area (in Poland, a voivodship, or region), in which the company[101] operates. Therefore, at the 'meso' level of airport operation there are primarily such issues to deal with as: the importance and attractiveness of regions or cities; issues of the location of the regional airport in relation to large agglomerations; as well as cooperation with regional authorities and stakeholders in the development of air transport system in the region (such as ROT, the Regional Tourism Organization). It is also worth noting the sectoral conditions resulting from the specifics of the air transport industry.

The micro-environment, as previously mentioned, sometimes also called the competitive environment, determines the actual competitive situation of the company. For an airport, the competitive environment is composed of other airports, as well as other entities: carriers (both traditional airlines and LCCs i.e. Low Cost Carriers), providers of transport services (e.g. handling agents), or companies offering substitute services (e.g. high speed trains).

The above-mentioned factors, as well as processes and mechanisms taking place within them, determine the functioning of the port, shape its policies and influence the actions taken by the management of individual airports. Therefore, it is necessary to single out the determinants, systematize and group them, and then determine how different factors affect the development of the airport – that is, to diagnose the direction and strength of their influence. The next step is to distinguish the domain of internal determinants of an airport and analyse its actual functioning.

The success of an airport relates to the port itself, seen as a profit-oriented business entity. However, we should be aware of its basic functions and the role it plays as a point infrastructure facility, serving air transportation system. The basic infrastructure to provide adequate traffic capacity is of primary importance for ports.[102] To provide proper facilities, space and equipment for the improvement of safety can be a considerable challenge for

---

mental segment in the macro-environment of companies. M. Bednarczyk, *Otoczenie i przedsiębiorczość...*, op. cit., p. 47.

[101] Eadem, *Organizacje publiczne...*, op. cit., pp. 95–102.

[102] Of importance are also indicators of airport capacity, which result from various factors – slot assignment or infrastructural facilities. It is essential that the airport is equipped with such elements as: the size of the airport capacity, the number of terminals, the number of runways, hangars, gates, sleeves, baggage systems, door systems, and security (monitoring system, electronic gates, scanners, etc.).

some airports.[103] Therefore, it is assumed that the main factors determining the competitive advantage of the port infrastructure are those that allow it to handle the right amount of passengers and cargo, as well as those that help ensure high quality of service provided. Equally important are managerial actions concerning quality, marketing, and safety policy.

3.2. Measures for the assessment of airport operation

The identification of key success factors consists in checking how the company is doing in comparison with its competitors. Evaluation of a given entity is based on the diagnosis of its competence, resources and strengths. Exemplary measures of air transport assessment are summarized in Figure 6.

Some of the listed measures allow performance assessment of the port's operations reflecting its competitive position (i.e. the outputs of the model; among others the per cent market share in passenger transport or freight transport, or the profit generated by the airport). An airport's competitive position is determined by its competitive potential, and the efficient use of that potential; and these elements – i.e. the inputs of the model – can be measured using appropriate indicators. So the procedure to identify significant determinants of airport competitiveness boils down to looking for significant correlations between factors constituting the potential of the competitive port (i.e. inputs) and the results achieved by the airport, showing their competitive position (i.e. outputs), while taking into account the efficient use of the former.

It is necessary to develop a method that would allow the assessment of the impact of qualitative and quantitative factors on the competitive position of Polish airports, the subset of which might be later considered as important determinants of competitiveness of the examined objects. In order to achieve this, adequate empirical evidence concerning Polish airports and their environments has to be gathered. A detailed method adopted for the conduct of this research will be discussed in chapter five of this monograph. The remaining part of this chapter presents research approaches applied in this regard.

---

[103] It is particularly important to have the right equipment in the ILS system, for flights cancelled due to bad weather conditions are a major disadvantage. Similarly adverse are delays resulting from the need to ensure safety (passport control, customs and quarantine requirements may cause delays in servicing passenger traffic). Strengthening security poses a number of problems, since it requires more personnel, additional equipment and larger terminal area. P. Forsyth, "The Impacts of Emerging Aviation Trends on Airport Infrastructure," *Journal of Air Transport Management* 13, 2007, pp. 45–52.

Figure 6. Basic performance metrics of air transport

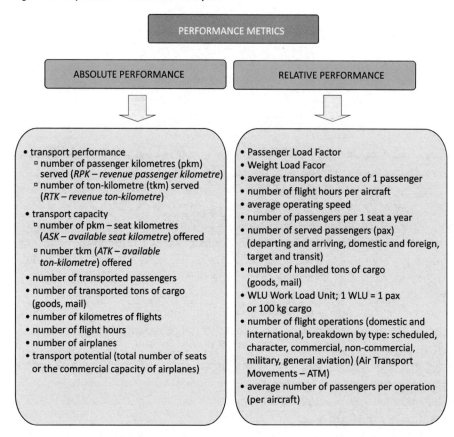

Source: own study based on D. Kaliński, *Zarządzanie organizacjami lotniczymi. Ekonomiczna charakterystyka usług lotnictwa cywilnego*, materiały szkoleniowe, Wydział Lotnictwa i OP Akademii Obrony Narodowej, 2007.

3.3. Selected methods for the analysis of competitiveness versus possible identification of the determinants of airport competitiveness

A set of methods and tools allowing the assessment of the competitive potential and competitive position, as well as assisting in strategic decision-making concerning competitiveness of the company, has been developed within the area referred to as 'competitive intelligence'.

The competitive intelligence (CI) is broadly defined as activities aimed at identifying, collecting, analysing and distributing knowledge on products, customers, competitors and regulation of all aspects of the environment needed to support essential decision-making for the organization.[104] According to this definition, the strategic competitive intelligence is a broader concept than the competition analysis, which is limited to gathering information on competitors and the processing of that information into useful knowledge for the company, using appropriate tools and methods.

Actions taken within the framework of competitive intelligence are aimed at solving a strictly defined problem (KIT – key intelligence topic) – in other words, the source, scope and manner of data collection and analytical methods are closely associated with the KIT. Thus, often instead of or in addition to public data from sources such as statistical authorities or repositories of corporate financial statements, unstructured data is used, consistent with the knowledge of experts, the findings obtained during trade fairs, trade or scientific conferences, results of scientific research, technological data, or data on contractors, clients, regulations and other aspects of the company's environment, coming from digital sources.

It is necessary for the purpose of analysing the company's competitiveness to merge data sets from different sources within one database, which can then be used to properly search (query) and analyse data relevant to solving a given problem, most commonly associated with a particular decision. The applicable method of analysis of the obtained data is also associated with well-defined problem, usually a decision-making one. The choice of specific analytical tools is determined by the purpose of competitive intelligence in a given company. Thus, ad hoc methods are often created, which are either modifications of the basic versions of established analytical methods, or methods combining elements of several analytical techniques.

One possible objective of competitive intelligence may be identifying important determinants of competitiveness and their impact on the competitive position of an entity – in this case, of an airport. The knowledge about relevant determinants of competitiveness of the airport, their nature and the extent to which they can be shaped by the company, will enable a better decision-making (both tactical and strategic), which will in turn affect its competitive position.

---

[104] C.S. Fleisher, D.L. Blenkhorn, *Management of Global Competitive Intelligence: the Way Ahead*, pp. 271–284 [in:] D.L Blenkhorn, C.S. Fleisher (eds.), *Competitive Intelligence and Global Business*, Westport, CT, Praeger Publishers, 2005; K. Tyson, *The Complete Guide to Competitive Intelligence*, 2nd ed., Leading Edge Publications, Chicago 2002; C. Murphy, *Competitive Intelligence: Gathering, Analysing and Putting It to Work*, Gower Publishing, Hampshire 2005. For Polish conditions, a model of analysis of competitiveness for small and medium-sized companies was presented by M. Bednarczyk in the work: *Otoczenie i przedsiębiorczość...*op. cit., pp. 87–95, and for public organizations: eadem, *Organizacja publiczna...*, op. cit., pp. 103–134.

The issue of competitive intelligence for an airport has become a research subject relatively recently, and the literature in this area started providing relevant publications only for some time now. Initial studies were conducted by Doganis and Graham (1987), who have been using different indicators to examine the workload unit (WLU) of selected European airports.[105] Graham (1998) revised the view of the earlier evaluation of airport performance dating from 1987.[106] And in 1989, Assailly conducted an analysis of French airports based on their performance.[107]

Among the most common methods used within the strategic competitive analysis of the company, typical, standard and commonly known methods of analysis are being applied such as SWOT analysis, Porter models, competitive benchmarking, PEST and STEEP,[108] expert methods, as well as statistical models, data mining tools and models (including Text Mining, and Web Mining).

Later in the monograph, methods and tools developed within competitive intelligence will be presented, which make it possible – on their own or in combination with other methods – to single out the factors determining the competitiveness of an airport.

Porter's five forces model

Every company – also an airport – operates in a particular external and internal environment, which is its source of opportunities, but also threats. The main objective of this method is to determine the competitive position of an airport, which can be measured according to the following sequence of actions:[109]

- determining the measurement criteria (identifying key success factors),
- weighted assessment of the selected criteria,
- assessment of the degree to which the selected factors have been mastered and a comparison with the achievements of competitors,
- collective assessment.

---

[105] R. Doganis, A. Graham, *The Role of Performance Indicators. Polytechnic of Central London*, Airport Management, London 1987.

[106] A. Graham, *Airport Economics and Performance Measurement*, Airport Economics and Finance Symposium University of Westminster, London 1998.

[107] C. Assailly, *Airport Productivity. An Analytical Study*, Institute of Air Transport, Paris 1989.

[108] Methods of assessment of company's environment PEST (political – P, economic – E, social – S, technological – T) and STEEP (S – social, T – technological, E – economic, E – environmental, P – political).

[109] Strategor, *Zarządzanie firmą*, Polskie Wydawnictwo Ekonomiczne, Warszawa 2001, p. 68.

The competitive position of an enterprise is usually characterized in a structural configuration of Porter's five forces analysis. It is a sectoral analysis, which is why it is so important to territorially isolate the sector. The objectives of sectoral analysis include: evaluating the attractiveness of the examined sector for the company and potential investors; ranking the sectors in which the company operates, according to development opportunities; searching for new sectors for the company's operations; estimating the cost of entering and exiting the sector. According to this concept, the competitive standing of the company depends on five basic 'forces':

- the power of influence of suppliers (the bargaining power of suppliers),
- the power of influence of buyers (the bargaining power of buyers),
- intensity of internal competitive rivalry (barriers to entering and exiting the sector),
- threat of new entrants (current rivals of the company),
- threat of substitute products.

Porter's five forces analysis is focused primarily on the strategic analysis of enterprises' competitiveness, given their microenvironment or sectoral specifics. It has been used in defining the competitiveness of Asian airports in 2003. In an interesting concept developed by Y. Park, the competitive advantage of an airport depends on 'five key factors', which can refer both to passenger and freight transport operations:[110]

- spatial qualities – the level of development of the regional airport, e.g. the presence of international trade zones, logistics and convention centres, aviation-related industrial complexes and other facilities;
- facilities – level of infrastructure of the airport and expansion of facilities in the existing airport in order to increase its capacity;
- demand – the level of demand depending on starting point and final destination, the demand and transit as well as traffic transfer, and the possibility of *hub-and-spoke* network development;
- service – level of service for users; types of operations at the airport; and fees;
- management – economic aspects, e.g. the airport's operating costs, productivity and revenue structure.

The main purpose of the airport competitiveness model is to determine factors favourable to the development of the airport and such that are

---

[110] Y. Park, "An Analysis for the Competitive Strength of Asian Major Airports," *Journal of Air Transport Management* 9, 2003, pp. 353–360.

hampering this development. Then an analysis of key success factors as well as factors deciding about failure has to be carried out. In this monograph we conduct an overview, followed by the comparative analysis and examination of groups of criteria, which are deemed the most important and decisive when it comes to competitive position and development opportunities of a company, in this case, an airport.

In order to obtain the confirmation regarding the importance of individual factors' impact on competitiveness, adequately constructed quantitative measures have been applied.

Econometric models

Based on a specified econometric model it is possible, with the help of statistical tests, to determine the significance and the impact of certain features on competitiveness, and more precisely, its aspects, measured using specific indicators. Features having a statistically significant effect on a certain level of airport competitiveness are considered to be its determinants.

An important element of the model building process is to adequately determine the dependent variable (or variables). The measuring scale of the dependent variables and their variation ranges (unlimited or limited) determines the type and class of applicable models.

The selection of a feature (or features), which might play the role of the dependent variable that is a measure of the level of competitiveness of the airport, may be derived from the (previously quoted) output measures, which serve to quantify the competitive position of the given entity.

Determining the competitive position of an entity should be multidimensional. If we are restricted to one output aspect of competitiveness (e.g. the share of individual airports in the passenger transport market in Poland as the dependent variable), the analysis of the impact of certain characteristics on its formation comes down to assessing the factors, which create the volumes of air passenger traffic.

For example, in the work by Dobruszkes et al. (2011)[111] an assessment was made of the impact on the volume of passenger traffic in the airport of such features as: the population of the area serviced by the port (catchment area); the GDP of the area (both features logarithmised); the distance of the airport from the nearest aviation market; the the volume of tourist traffic in the area served by the port; the development of R&D sector in the region; the scope of economic decisions taken in the region; and international administrative functions of the region (the last three qualities evaluated in a point rating).

---

[111] F. Dobruszkes et al., "An Analysis of the Determinants of Air Traffic Volume for European Metropolitan Areas," *Journal of Transport Geography* 19, 2011, pp. 755–762.

The model's dependent variable was the volume of passenger traffic at the port. Empirical material consisted of cross-sectional data from 131 European airports. The following determinants were deemed important for the size of air traffic in European ports (within stepwise linear regression): the GDP of the area; the scope of economic decisions taken in the region; the volume of tourist traffic in the area; and the distance between the port and the nearest aviation market. These features were jointly responsible for 70% of the variance of the dependent variable.

Another thread of research on the subject is dealing with evaluating the factors, which determine the choice of particular airports by individual passengers. In this case, a qualitative trait is assumed as a model explanatory variable, in which individual categories correspond to the choice of the port by the passenger. Due to the nature of the dependent variable, a logit model (binary trait – two airports) or polynomial logit model (polychotomous feature – more than two airports) is used – among others, socio-demographic characteristics of passengers and the distance from the passenger's place of residence to the port were applied. Such studies were conducted for airports situated in one metropolitan area (multi-airport urban region), for example in San Francisco,[112] through surveying the port's passengers. They made it possible to determine the nature of competitiveness of various ports and their area of specialization.

The abovementioned formulas of examination focused on a selected aspect of an airport's competitiveness. In the case of Polish airports, econometric modelling of the competitive position in a multidimensional approach is more difficult, due to both formal and empirical obstacles. Many of the consequential aspects of competitive position are difficult to quantify (e.g. the position of the brand and the tradition of the company), which is an enormous challenge in this kind of research. Even if – due to the limited number of airports in Poland – we were to restrict our area of studies (admittedly rendering the analysis far more vague) to adopting only one dependent variable, namely the share of individual ports in passenger traffic, the construction of a model capable of selecting and assessing the level of impact of various factors influencing the competitiveness based on cross-sectional data (i.e. from one period) would not be possible.

In the case of collecting more cross-sectional data (e.g. for European airports), due to the fact that the dependent variable – the share in the passenger transport market of each port – has a value in the range of $<0, 1>$ (which for

[112] An example of such studies for airports from San Francisco metropolitan area can be found in: G. Başar, C. Bhat, "A Parameterized Consideration Set Model for Airport Choice. An Application to the San Francisco Bay Area," Transportation Research Part B Methodological Volume 38, Issue 10, 2004.

the considered group of ports should add up to one), a fractional multinominal logit[113] model could be used. This model is analogous to a polynomial logit model, but with a difference that in the former case the role of the dependent variable was taken by the feature representing the percentage of occurrence of a given category (in this case the percentage of passengers who used a given port, i.e. the share of the airport in the passenger transport market), and in the later case, the dependent is a qualitative polynomial variable, the values of which represent specific categories.

For the study of Polish airports, the application of panel data could also be considered – data set would comprise the observations of Polish airports in the coming years. However, the estimator of the parameters of the fractional logit model used for cross-sectional data in case of longitudinal data is overloaded, which requires the usage of another estimator, for which in turn it is necessary to use a large sample for correct inference (the asymptotic properties of the estimator are used). This fact can be a hindrance, because the Polish data concerning airports is available only for a relatively small number of time periods in the past.

In econometric models, there also exist some restrictions concerning the use of qualitative characteristics in the role of explanatory variables and the number of categories assumed by them; furthermore, there is no possibility to include hard-to-measure aspects that may explain the development of competitiveness of an airport.

One possible way of overcoming the aforementioned obstacles is to use a different approach for measuring the significance of the impact of various factors on the competitive position of the unit.

An alternative group of methods to facilitate the determination of factors significantly influencing the competitiveness (competitive position) of an airport and the various elements showing the competitive potential of entities are those methods, which apply indirect measurement, based on expert indications concerning the degree of significance of a given factor on a properly constructed measuring scale. The indirectness of the measurement consists in creating a scale (a ranking scale or such for relative measurements) for the experts' indications, the values from which are then subjected to the corresponding transformations in order to get the final measure of the perceived significance of individual features' impact on the airport's competitiveness (possibly in the form of scales, indicative of the significance of the impact of individual features).

---

[113] A formal model description with application example can be found in the following work: P.F. Koch, "Fractional Multinomial Response Models with an Application to Expenditure Shares," *University of Pretoria Working Paper* 21, 2010.

Benchmark analysis – a review of empirical research

One of the methods allowing a comparison of entities with regard to the level of their competitiveness and their ranking position in this regard is benchmarking in its many varieties.

Benchmark analysis is one of the most important instruments used to assess the performance of airport infrastructure management, and its popularisation was due to advancing processes of privatization and commercialization in the air services sector. Benchmarking allows comparative studies of the effective use of the competitive potential of a given airport, taking into account the changes occurring in the air transport market.

The main idea behind benchmarking is a creative imitation of the best type of solution, which then leads to improving and adapting within the scope of one's own need, as it refers to a benchmark (reference point, standard, model) or best practice (creative imitation).[114] There are many definitions of benchmarking, but all of them underline such features as: continuity, improvement, learning from others, and applying best practices.

Benchmarking can be used to identify different areas of airport operations, ranging from passenger satisfaction, quality of service, comparison of the efficiency of ground operations, to examining the relationship between quality of service and the level of costs. Proper evaluation of the performance of air operations can provide valuable reference, which can be helpful in decision-making related to investments.

Airport benchmarking is viewed as a complex issue, which is associated with diverse contributions and differences in expenditures made, as well as with a sophisticated business environment of individual airports. Airport executives are increasingly more focused on the problems of air operations, and they are looking for opportunities to improve their performance (comparative analysis). Changes in the management of airports are additionally reinforced by the crisis caused by terrorist attacks of 9/11, as well as by the financial crisis and the associated pressures coming from business environments to reduce costs.

The most pertinent benchmarking variety – in terms of studies that are concerned with finding the factors, which determine competitiveness of an airport, and the method of assessing the effectiveness of these factors in comparison with competitors – is competitive benchmarking.

---

[114] In general, the benchmark is a point of reference – a model, and it is most commonly defined as a method 'to analyse the achievements of companies with reference to particular success factor and the search for the common reference base that would enable it to significantly improve them.'

Within competitive benchmarking, in order to evaluate the efficiency of realizing the competitive potential of an airport, it is possible to apply the DEA method (Data Envelopment Analysis). DEA facilitates the assessment of the effectiveness of transforming outlays (input, in this case, the factors that determine the competitive potential), into outputs, or factors determining the competitive position of the port, while taking into account existing capabilities (empirically defined technologies of transforming inputs into outputs for the group of examined entities). In the case of the output-oriented DEA method, for each examined company from the group equipped with the same technology of transforming inputs into outputs, a coefficient is set with the value from the range <0, 1>, indicating the proportion relative to the current engagement of inputs, and guaranteeing a fixed level of outputs. Companies for which the coefficient equals 1 are fully technically efficient (at a given level of performance, they effectively use their inputs). Among others, the following rule applies: the closer to 1 the efficiency coefficient is, the higher the efficiency of the inputs used. On the basis of the set values of the efficiency coefficients, the companies from the given group can be ranked according to the decreasing value of the designated coefficient – the lower the coefficient in the range <0, 1>, the lower the efficiency of the inputs. However, in the DEA method it is necessary to identify the features in the accepted model of inputs (factors that represent competitive potential) and effects (factors that measure the competitive position of the company), which should be determined by other methods, such as the aforementioned expert methods.[115]

Benchmark studies concerning airports are carried out in a multifaceted way on varying levels of complexity, depending on the set goals and the needs of clients – the entities, for which such studies are being carried out.

Airport benchmarking can be beneficial for many entities that have a vested interest in the development of airports. These are for example: airport management companies, central administrative bodies, local authorities, regional authorities, construction companies, developers, regional development agencies, service and product providers for airports, consultancies, or academic centres. In an attempt to classify these entities, we can distinguish the following stakeholder groups:

---

[115] It must be stressed that not all levels of inputs (that is, factors shaping the competitive potential of an entity) undergo random changes, which may be taken into account by use of a variety of the DEA method (*project-controlled multi-objective DE*). An example of application of two DEA approaches mentioned in this subchapter can be found in: J.C. Guan et al., "A study of Relationship between Competitiveness and Technological Innovation Capability Based on DEA Models," *European Journal of Operational Research* 170, 2006, pp. 971–986.

- airport boards of directors – benchmark analyses give them the possibility to identify and adapt best practices already used by their competitors, and thus provide an opportunity to improve productivity and efficiency;
- airlines – interested in operating at efficient, well-managed airports, offering their services at competitive prices;
- municipal authorities – interested in efficient and effective operations of an airport on their territory; as it attracts capital and tourists, and also increases the availability of air services for local population. This is particularly important in cases where municipal authorities are part owners of an airport;
- federal and state authorities – interested in the results of benchmark analyses especially in terms of international comparisons, useful for the development of transportation policy and infrastructure in the given country;
- investors and shareholders – interested to know which ports are worth investing in and which will bring the greatest benefits;
- aviation market regulators – benchmarking studies are interesting for them in terms of influencing service quality levels, price regulation and general business conditions.[116]

Airport benchmarking has been adopted in the past 15 years, thanks to the fact that many regional airports in Poland have moved from under direct control of the public sector to the private-public sector. Liberalisation, commercialization, and globalization of the aviation industry have contributed to the economic growth of airports, their complexity and competitiveness, generating the need for creating performance indicators. Many airports have adopted aggressive business philosophy and practices aimed at raising the profile of airport services and their performance. Through the use of benchmarking, airport operators are up to date when it comes to monitoring the data obtained from benchmarking indicators, and comparing their airport with other airports in order to improve efficiency.[117]

---

[116] V. Kamp, H.M. Niemeir, *Benchmarking of German Airports – Some First Results and Agenda for Further Research*, www.gap-projekt.de (access: 10.07.2014), p. 14. The issue of the use of benchmark analysis by managing directors or managers of airports has been described in the following article: G. Francis, I. Humphreys, J. Fry, "The Benchmarking of Airport Performance," *Journal of Air Transport Management* 8, 2002, pp. 239–247.

[117] A. Graham, "Airport Benchmarking: A Review of the Current Situation," *Benchmarking: An International Journal* 12(2), 2005, pp. 99–111.

Quantitative analysis of significant influencing factors shaping competitiveness of an airport based on expert assessments

In view of the fact that many of the features that may have a potential impact on the competitiveness of an airport are hard to measure and they cannot be directly included in an econometric model, a thread of research was developed that uses the measure of significance of different features based on expert assessment.

Special scales are being constructed to assess significant influencing features as perceived by experts, giving evidence of the competitive potential of an entity to shape its competitive position (results). It should be noted that the measurement of the perceived level of significance of particular features is done indirectly, through the appropriate transformation of ratings indicated by experts on the scale adopted in the questionnaire. Suitable transformations allow for measuring errors resulting from human perception.

In practice, a questionnaire is being drawn up in which experts assess the impact of individual characteristics of any nature – qualitative or quantitative (including also those for which a quantitative measurement may pose difficulties) from a list of features, prepared by an expert, which may affect the development of the studied entity's competitiveness. It is also possible to first assess the significance of the influence of a group of related features, and then the individual feature from the previously composed groups (hierarchical approach).

For expert assessment, a ranking scale (e.g. Likert scale) can be adopted, or relative scales with pairwise comparisons used in the AHP method (Analytic Hierarchy Process). And so, in the case of using a Likert scale for expert assessment (evaluation from 1 to 5) in order to obtain measurements – weights from a continuous scale, corresponding to the perceived significance of the influence of the considered features upon competitiveness – a Rating Scale Model[118] can be used, which is an expansion of Rasch model[119] in case of answers determined on an ordinal scale (it is also possible to use fuzzy Rasch model – you receive fuzzy weights of the significance of perceived features). However, in the case of using the relative scale with pairwise comparisons (known from AHP method) for the expert assessments, experts estimate the perceived significant influence on the competitiveness of the entity of one feature, compared to significant effect of another feature (typically for the

---

[118] Model introduced by D. Andrich, "A Rating Formulation for Ordered Response Categories," *Psychometrika* 43(4), 1978, pp. 561–573.

[119] Description of Rasch model can be found in the following work: G. Rasch, *Probabilistic Models for Some Intelligence and Attainment Tests*, Danish Institute for Educational Research, Copenhagen 1960.

relative ratings, integers from 1 to 9 and their inverses are applied).[120] And so comparisons are made for all possible pairs of evaluated features. Relative assessments of the significant influence of the features are collected in a square matrix, the diagonal values of which are equal to 1, and the symmetric values with respect to the diagonal are their own inverses. In the case of acceptably low inconsistency coefficient (for a maximum threshold, coefficient value of [0.1] is assumed), previously standardized values of the first vector of said matrix are taken as the weight of significant influencing features (referred to in AHP as the potentials).

In the case of assuming a relative scale for expert assessments, it is possible to take hierarchical levels into account – for example, upper layer consisting of groups of related features, and lower layer consisting of the specific features relating to the group. Firstly an assessment of relative level of significant influence on the entity's competitiveness is carried out for compiled pairs of features. Then, within each group, comparisons are made relative to the significance of individual features.

With the use of weights determined based on the methods shown above, it is possible to create synthetic measurements, allowing for ordering units due to the level of their competitiveness. An important step in this approach is the creation of corresponding list of features by the expert (including the possible division into groups) that may affect the competitiveness of the entity, the significance of which will be measured by the expert. In order to create a list of potentially relevant aspects (features) affecting the competitiveness of an airport, it may be useful to compile a diagram for dividing the features according to their origin (Figure 7).

Use of analytical scheme in the study of airport competitiveness

Based on the previously presented assumptions about the competitiveness of an airport and the impact of the environment, an attempt was made to develop a research model of competitiveness. The use of analytical scheme[121] in the

---

[120] Such approach has been applied in: G.I. Crouch, "Modelling Destination Competitiveness: a Survey and Analysis of the Impact of Competitiveness Attributes," *CRC for Sustainable Tourism*, 2007.

[121] An analytical scheme is one of the basic cognitive-methodological categories in economic sciences and broadly in social sciences. To summarize extensive discussion on this subject in the literature, we can conclude that the analytical scheme is a research tool consisting in determining the essential characteristics or variables describing a given phenomenon, process or a specified theoretical category and in more complicated view – apart from the identification of variables aiming at defining the variability of these variables and outlining directions of dependencies between them. Source: M. Gorynia, *Luka konkurencyjna na poziomie przedsiębiorstwa a przystąpienie Polski do Unii Europejskiej*, Wydawnictwo Akademii Ekonomicznej w Poznaniu, Poznań 2002, pp. 11–17.

Figure 7. Interdependencies between various elements of the airport's environment

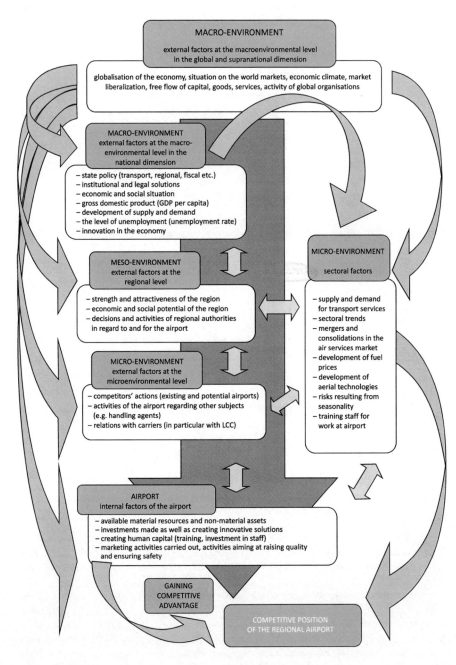

Source: own study.

development of airport competitiveness aims to include major groups of factors that have a significant impact on determining the competitive position of the port. The success or failure of an airport depends on its competitiveness. Measures aimed at examining competitiveness of an airport are derivative, and as a consequence of the above statement, they constitute a great challenge for the company, in this case, an airport. A visualisation of the most important areas to be evaluated and their components, with a potential impact on the competitive standing of the airport, is shown in Figure 7. The diagram shows interactions between different spheres, and it aims to illustrate the selected key elements and conditions emerging from individual layers of the environment. It also takes into account endogenous factors, inherent to the internal structures of airports.

It should be noted that strong interactions take place between environmental factors (macro-, meso- and micro-). They create mechanisms, regulations and processes that shape the functional framework of a regional airport. The obvious fact is that as a consequence of the changing political, economic or social conditions, there is a noticeable change of circumstances in other spheres and planes that form the framework for the functioning of a given airport.[122]

It can be stated that there are different levels of competitiveness, with which a Polish regional airport must come to terms and this is the subject matter of this monograph. We need to consider the fact that the key determinants of competitiveness of modern enterprises are of interactive character, and that they are in fact a combination of factors creating a multi-dimensional space. They should not be seen as single isolated variables, but rather in terms of a set of interdependent elements that appear in the same time frame and permeate each other. This approach stresses the effect of their combined impact on the competitiveness of the company, which finds confirmation in management practice.[123] It is also worth noting that these considerations do not exhaust the complexity of the issues in question, but the presented model

---

[122] The impact of the euro on the competitiveness of businesses may, for example, be both direct and indirect. The indirect impact will happen through changes in the widely considered business environment, in particular in relations between companies and institutions from financial and insurance sector, but also in changes in the macroeconomic data describing the state of the economy. By contrast, the direct impact is connected with an effect on the competitive position occupied by the company, its competitive potential and the applied competitive strategy by the company, which consists of and which is being determined by functional strategies implemented. Source: M. Gorynia, B. Jankowska, M. Pietrzykowski, P. Tarka, M. Dzikowska, "Przystąpienie Polski do strefy euro a międzynarodowa konkurencyjność i internacjonalizacja polskich przedsiębiorstw," *Ekonomista* 4, 2011, pp. 471–491.

[123] W. Walczak, "Niematerialne determinanty konkurencyjności współczesnych przedsiębiorstw" [in:] *Konkurencyjność jako determinanta rozwoju przedsiębiorstwa*, eds. P. Lachiewicz, M. Matejun, Wydawnictwo Politechniki Łódzkiej, Łódź 2009, pp. 112–115.

reflects the actual circumstances and processes in business practice. It can also be a starting point for further in-depth analyses in the context of separate specific research problems. Each company should individually consider the outlined interdependencies and connections due to the fact that the specific characteristics of a given industry will always decide which factors have the greatest impact.[124]

Several important issues deserve attention in the constructed model:

- competitiveness of an airport will be treated ex-post, i.e. the competitive position as a result of the synergistic interaction of an integrated group of interconnected external and internal factors and measures undertaken by the company;
- competitiveness of modern airports depends directly on the conditions and determinants of competitiveness for this sector and is influenced by the economic situation in the country and the situation in the world markets;
- airport's capability for undertaking measures to improve the level of competitiveness (improving the competitive position) depends significantly on factors occurring in its environment;
- gaining competitive advantage may be the result of offering distinctive products and services, but also the result of political and business arrangements and connections thanks to profitable orders or public contracting.[125]

Competitive position of a regional airport is a result of multi-faceted conditions, relationships and activities undertaken by the company. Airports are influenced by both the overall economic standing of the country, and the global economic situation. All these factors have a direct impact on the port, while they also influence each other – directly or indirectly, they determine the development of a given airport.[126] The direct influence of the company on

---

[124] For the construction of multimodal model, forces were used to analyse the competitiveness of airports based on an assessment of all elements grouped in a given ratio according to the position method in the ranking, the total assessment of each group coefficient, and also mean values for each coefficient were taken into account.

[125] These include, among others: connections, unfair tenders, political and business ties and connections, which cause one company to greatly increase its competitiveness, yielding measurable financial benefits. These factors can be described as 'outstanding' abilities to shape business relationships with selected stakeholders, who have appropriate powers in particular to issue administrative decisions and who administer financial resources.

[126] For example, the development of a regional airport is heavily dependent on environmental conditions and this in turn is linked to its location, but it should be remembered that environmental requirements arise from legal environment created at both national and international level.

the competitive environment varies, and depends on its competitive strength shaped by the applied competitive strategy.

The competitiveness of an analysed entity – a Polish regional airport – is thus a derivative of influencing factors from various segments of the external environment and the actions of the port itself. We should consider the current competitive position of an entity, but also the potential competitive position, without forgetting the threat of substitutive competition. Of course, such an analysis must be applied to specific cases, with reference to the situation on the transnational scale, and it must take into account both current and future forecasts concerning the development of the market for services offered by airports.

4. EXTERNAL AND INTERNAL DETERMINANTS OF REGIONAL AIRPORT COMPETITIVENESS

The success or failure of such enterprise depends on determinants, which should be examined as an impact of various external and internal factors. The multiplicity of these elements, as well as diverse strength of their impact, cause the study of determinants of the development of regional airport and their effect on its competitiveness – possible success or failure – to be a very complex process.

In the first section of this chapter, we will present the external determinants affecting the activity of Polish airports. The (external) environment of an airport is an outside source of its competitiveness and a source of both possibilities (opportunities) and threats (restrictions) to the growth of the port. The basis for the development strategy, that is strategic port competitiveness, is to identify the most important factors in the different layers of the environment i.e. macro-, meso- and micro-environment. The operation and competition of the airport is shaped by strong interactions, which occur between various elements of the environment (macro-, meso- and micro-).[127]

At the micro-environment level, the regional airport is impacted by factors related to the fact that the facility operates in specific global conditions, although it exists in a particular region and country. It is also significantly influenced by the general socio-demographic situation. Among the most significant determinants at meso-environment level are factors related to the issue of attractiveness of cities and regions (the strength of the region and its economic and social potential, etc.). Micro-level is defined as the so-called direct (competitive) environment of the regional airport, therefore it includes sets of factors relating to the relevant geographic market, the airport's location or its place in the intermodal freight transport system. It is particularly important to look at the range of impact (*catchment area*) of Polish regional airports against adjacent major ports, especially in Germany.

---

[127] Due to the complexity of undertaken research, the more significant elements are described thoroughly, while other, less important are merely mentioned.

The ability to meet challenges resulting from all spheres of the external environment essentially influences the development of the competitive position of the regional airport. What matters is whether its attitude will be passive or active, whether the opportunities will be seized and crisis situations will be eliminated. Airport Management Board's skills to take firm actions are also highly significant. Therefore, in the second section of the chapter, the internal determinants of regional airport competitiveness will be discussed.

4.1. Macro-, meso- and micro-environment factors determining the competitive position of a regional airport

Specificity of the macro-environment of an airport

Each airport is affected by many factors related to its geographical and geopolitical location, however the phenomena constituting the macro-environment of the port are both global and regional. This group of factors is very complex and indirectly touches different spheres of life.

While examining the macro-factors, which determine the development of an airport, demographic, socio-cultural and technological determinants have to be taken into account. Currently, environmental issues and matters relating to security are becoming increasingly important. Along with the aforementioned determinants, airports must deal with many unusual events, which may be seen as an opportunity for its development, or a threat thereto. However, in the discussion of the airport macro-environment, macroeconomic determinants seem to be the most important, and these determinants should be considered first by the persons responsible for the growth of an airport.

Economic development of any country is closely correlated with the improvement of air transport infrastructure and thus its ability to participate in the creation of GDP and to provide employment opportunities.[128] The state of the economy influences the development of the volume of air traffic, both passenger and freight services. In turn, the volume of traffic conditions the intensity of activities by the airlines activities, which are the main clients of the airports.

---

[128] From the European perspective, it should be noted that the whole transport sector employs over 10 million people, which constitutes 4.5% of the employees in total, and produces 4.6% of GDP. Manufacture of transport equipment is responsible for another 1.7% of GDP and 1.5% of employment. Airports and airlines in the EU employ 670 thousand people and approximately 3.2 million people are directly or indirectly dependent on the air transport sector. Source: European Commission, *Impact Assessment of the Single Aviation Market on employment and working conditions for the period 1997-2007*, Brussels 2010 , pp. 4–5. http://ec.europa.eu/transport/modes/air/internal_market/doc/sec_2010_503_en.pdf (access: 10.08.2014).

Meso-environment factors determining the competitiveness of a regional airport

Even though properly conducted macroeconomic policy of the country determines its economic growth, it is not a sufficient condition for prosperity. The economic activity of enterprises and competitive conditions in which they operate still depend on many other factors, including the determinants and potential of the meso-environment, i.e. regional determinants.[129]

Meso-environment is referred to as an intermediate layer between macro- and micro-environment, where the influence of macro-environment is transferred into the micro-environment of the enterprise. Meso-environment is essentially an environment of the regional enterprise, for which two different perspectives were distinguished: subject-oriented and object-oriented. Subject-oriented perspective includes mainly groups affecting the operation of the airport in the area: governmental and local administration bodies, local tax offices, service entities and institutions supporting the development of entrepreneurship and business activity. Object-oriented perspective of meso-environment emphasizes local aspects of the macro-environment, in particular the level of economic development of the region and its attractiveness (e.g. investment, tourism) that affects the image of the region and sets out the direction of its promotion; the profile of the local labour market (the pool of highly skilled workers, the availability and quality of education and training); incomes of the population living in the region and the standard of living of local communities (e.g. local taxes); availability of capital and financial support; initiatives taken by the self-government for development of entrepreneurship; and transfer of knowledge and technology.

Regional airport functions as a service for residents and visitors to the region, thus its competitiveness depends to a large extent on the competitiveness of the region, which the port is serving.

Micro-environment factors of a regional airport's competitiveness

The airport is directly affected by its micro-environment, the so-called competitive environment. Entities and factors from the micro-environment level have an impact on the enterprise's operation, in this case, an airport, however the airport also shapes its surroundings. The extent, to which the port may have an impact on its environment at the micro level, depends on the

---

[129] More information on reviewing the classification of meso environment: M. Bednarczyk, *Otoczenie i przedsiębiorczość w zarządzaniu strategicznym organizacją gospodarczą*, Zeszyty Naukowe Akademii Ekonomicznej w Krakowie, Seria Specjalna: Monografie, Kraków 1996, pp. 46–49; K. Wach, "Mezootoczenie małych i średnich przedsiębiorstw w ujęciu czynnikowym," *Zeszyty Naukowe Uniwersytetu Ekonomicznego w Krakowie* 799, 2009, http://mpra.ub.uni-muenchen.de/31674/1/MPRA_paper_31674.pdf (access: 10.05.2014).

structure of supply (the number and market power of the airport's competitors), the structure of market demand (on the part of the airlines and passengers) and the competitive position of the airport within the market.

In economics, the micro-environment, also called a competitive (or direct) environment of the enterprise, comprises general economic and non-economic entities (specific organizations or groups) which directly affect the enterprise, and which may be directly affected by the enterprise. It conditions the functioning and development of the enterprise in a specific industry, sector or market segment. The competitive environment of the airport comprises all entities that, in the process of meeting customer needs, have a cooperative or a competitive relationship with the port (Figure 8).

Figure 8. Competitive environment of the regional airport

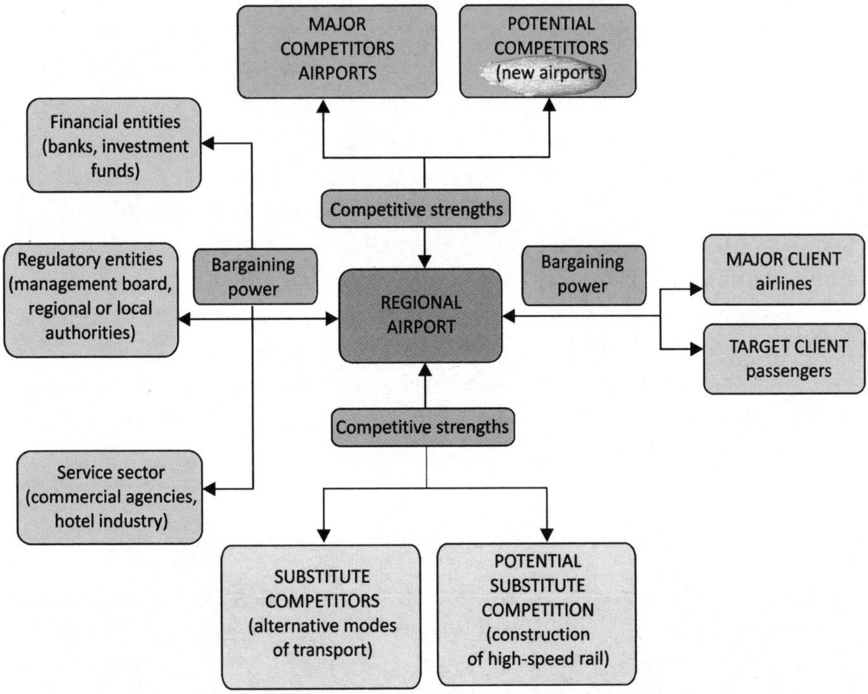

Source: own study.

The diagram highlights two basic types of relationships between entities in the competitive environment, referred to as bargaining power and competitive strength. Regarding the competitive strength, we should note the impact of direct competitors and substitute competitors. Direct competitors of the airport are the pre-existing airports or future airports, which may provide an alternative for the customers. Substitute competitors are enterprises, which offer transportation services related to alternative modes of transport.

The intensity of competition from direct competitors is conditioned, among others, by:

- number of competitors, their tangible and intangible potential;
- structure of the market share;
- market size and its growth rate;
- level of costs associated with the acquisition of customers from one competitor to another.

For the airport, which is one of the links in the chain of air transport services provision, the substitute competitors are transport service providers who use other modes of transportation (bus, rail, water). The choice of the mode of transport is determined by a comparison of the consumers' perceptions of the utility and costs associated with the use of the transport mode (e.g. distance to the destination and the duration of travel, comfort, direct and frequent connections).

In order to build, maintain and strengthen their competitive position, airports should properly and continuously research the market. In the sphere of demand, the spatial extent of the market for air transportation services, the so-called *catchment area*, must be recognized, as well as its personal scope – the main customers of ports are airlines, and the size of demand for airport services depends on the demand for airline services concerning passenger and freight transport to/from the area served by the port, and on the costs related to the use of the port. In terms of the structure of supply of the airport services market, it is important to identify the competitors of the airport, or other ports that may have an alternative way to meet the customers' demand. Substitute competitors, providers of transportation services using forms of transport other than air, should also be recognized. Barriers to competitors' market entry, including substitute competitors, are crucial.

The degree of competition between airports is limited due to the existence of the airport's natural monopoly, which, in turn, is connected with the existence of incumbent markets, i.e. airport facilities. Therefore, it is assumed that the overlapping *catchment areas* of neighbouring airports become a particularly important area of competition (see: Drawing 2).

The *catchment area* of an enterprise is defined as a territorial area from which customers are obtained[130] – in other words, it is the geographic scope

---

[130] The customer for the airport is understood as a passenger residing or living in the catchment area of the airport who uses services of airlines providing connections with the ones.

of the market, generating demand for goods or services of the enterprise. With access to information on the place of residence or origin of customers, the *catchment area* can be determined empirically, inter alia, by *data mining* techniques (e.g. using cluster analysis, especially the K-Means method).[131] Another way to establish the *catchment area* of the enterprise is to arbitrarily define it on the basis of an assumed set of criteria, such as e.g. travel time to the enterprise or affiliation to the particular administrative unit.

In the case of airports, when determining the *catchment area*, arbitrary approach is typically assumed, however the selection criteria depends on the needs. In a broader sense, the *catchment area* of the an airport is generally defined as the area from which you can reach the airport within two hours, that is a circle with a radius of about 100 km. Narrowly, it may be defined as the area from which you can reach the airport within 60 minutes, that is a circle with a radius of about 50 km[132] (see: Drawing 2).

In subject literature, it is assumed that significant competitive space of airports is provided by the overlapping *catchment areas* of adjacent airports. Therefore, all airports endeavour to expand their impact range. A particular increase in the intensity of competitive struggle takes place when areas of influence of neighbouring enterprises overlap. In this situation, in order to maintain or improve the competitive position, the airport should offer an attractive range of air services and connections adapted to consumers' preferences,[133] and ensure convenient access thereto.

Currently, there is a strong tendency to locate and modernize ports several kilometres away from the city centres, reducing travel time and providing more economical solution due to the use of existing urban infrastructure. In terms of social transportation efficiency, the distance to the airport should be approximately 7–20 km for local and continental traffic, and 20–35 km for transcontinental traffic. The possibility for accessible transport to/from the airport considerably increases the *catchment area* of the airport, i.e. the market of potential passengers using the airport expands, and this significantly affects the growth of its competitiveness.

---

[131] An example of the application of the k-means method to identify the catchment area of the hospital can be found in is given in: SJ. Gilmour, "Identification of Hospital Catchment Areas Using Clustering: An Example from the NHS," *Health Services Research* 45(2), 2010.

[132] http://www.champions-project.de/public_docs/CHAMPIONS%20Savaria,%20 West%20Pannon.pdf (access: 10.02.2014). The catchment area is also defined as isochrones or isolines with an average travel times of 60, 90 and 120 minutes. Source: "Civil Aviation Authority, Catchment Area Analysis," *Working Paper*, October 2011, p. 8.

[133] K. Fuellhart, "Airport Catchment and Leakage in a Multi-airport Region: The Case of Harrisburg International," *Journal of Transport Geography* 15, 2007, pp. 231–244; http://mkm. de/content_files/publications/airport_ choice_and_competition.pdf (access: 10.02.2014).

Drawing 2. *Catchment areas* of selected Polish airports

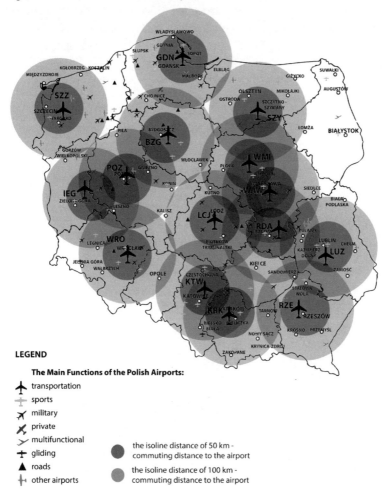

Source: own study.

We must bear in mind that formation of the demand structure, directly related to the *catchment area* of the airport, should be seen in particular
through the lens of regions, which cover the area of influence. These regions
are not homogeneous – they differ at least in terms of demographic potential,
economic development and productivity.

It will be useful to take a closer look at the structure of competitors for the
Polish airports. This will allow for a clearer description of the development
of supply structure and its future changes in the light of competitive rivalry
between the ports.

The airports' problem of competing for passengers appeared along with
the opening of the Polish market of aviation services.

Previously limited availability of airports and air services, strong domination of WAW airport and monopoly position of LOT Polish airlines, explicitly excluded the phenomenon of competition within the Polish market of aviation services. Polish ports, especially regional ones, began to compete against each other only as a result of the *open skies* policy – since 1 May 2004, the Polish market of air transport services is an integral part of the liberalized transport service market of the European Community.

Competition analysis of enterprises uses the so-called maps of strategic groups, since the space of strategic competition is created by direct competitors, coming from the same strategic group.[134] Map of the following strategic groups, including competitive ports, was drawn for each Polish airport. Here is a complete list of these groups:

- For WAW airport: KRK, KTW, WRO, LCJ as well as airports situated in Germany: Berlin – SXF and TXL (in the future, BER), Munich – MUC and in Prague – PRG and Vienna – VIE;
- For BZG airport: GDN as well as WAW, POZ, WRO;
- For GDN airport: BZG, SZZ, WAW, as well as an airport situated in the Kaliningrad District, Russia – KGD;
- For IEG airport: POZ, WRO;
- For KRK airport: KTW, RZE, WRO, as well as Poprad – Tatry airport located in Slovakia – TAT, Žilina, SLO – ILZ, – SLD, Ostrava in Czech Republic – OSR and Lviv, Ukraine – LWO;
- For KTW airport: KRK, WRO, WAW, LCJ, as well as Poprad – Tatry airport located in Slovakia –TAT, Žilina, SLO;
- For LCJ airport: WAW as well as KTW, WRO, POZ;
- For POZ airport: BZG, IEG as well as WRO, LCJ, SZZ,
- For RZE airport: KRK, KTW, as well as airports situated in Ukraine – Lviv – LWO, and Ivano-Frankivsk – IFO;
- For SZZ airport: BZG, GDN, as well as Berlin airports;
- For WRO airport: SZZ, POZ, WAW, as well as Berlin airports.

It will be interesting to observe the change in the situation of Polish airports after new, yet strong airports start their operation (e.g. the Modlin port), and to see the impact of the competition from Berlin airports on the Polish airports in Wrocław, Poznań and Szczecin.[135]

---

[134] Bednarczyk M., *Organizacje publiczne. Zarządzanie konkurencyjnością*, Wydawnictwo Naukowe PWN, Warszawa–Kraków 2001, p. 127.
[135] According to data from 2006, Berlin airports handled 18.6 million passengers, including about 2.3–2.6 million passengers from Poland, while in 2008 more than 2 million Poles had flown from Berlin, rather than using Polish airports and airlines. Central Airport planned as a hub for Poland, according to the assumptions does not threaten the regional airports,

Because a regional airport often plays the role of one stage in a multistage journey, usually the first or the last stop, particularly for long-haul flights, the functioning of the so-called hub ports is particularly important for Polish regional airports. Apart from Warsaw Chopin Airport (formerly Warsaw-Okęcie Airport), the nearest hubs are (mainly) Frankfurt and Munich. Under the conditions of European integration and the implementation of *open skies* policy, Polish airports also face stiff competition from other German ports, which try hard to win Polish passengers, e.g. Dresden and Leipzig. Thanks to growing cooperation with travel agencies, airports attract passengers with cheap travel packages, cheap airline tickets, transfer facilities to and from Poland, cheap and long-term parking, rich accommodation base and a high level of service at the airport and in its direct neighbourhood. Meanwhile, the countries across the Eastern border: Ukraine, Belarus, and even Romania and Bulgaria are potential markets for our aviation industry.

4.2. Internal determinants of a regional airport's competitiveness

Airports in Poland function mostly as commercial companies.[136] State Treasury and local government units are their main shareholders.[137] All airports carry out a lot of work to become a competitive force on the market but it is the aviation infrastructure that is the fundament of the airport's operation. It is on the basis of adequate infrastructure that the policy of quality and safety is shaped, and the scope of investments and marketing activities are determined. Speaking about the internal conditions of competitiveness of a regional airport, we should consider not only the current state of the airport's infrastructure and the strengths of the airport (resulting from his-

---

and is expected to contribute to the growth of the entire passenger traffic in Poland. Central Airport is to be a major transit hub, supporting other regions. Launch of new hub is an enormous investment. Construction of the entire system correlating domestic voyages with medium distance connections and long-haul flights is necessary. Therefore, the Central Airport is economically justified only as a base port (the interchange) of large carriers with already developed network of connections, especially long-haul. Source: *Mityczny BBI. Mityczny CPL* 2010-04-13, obtained from: http://www.prtl.pl/artykuly,245,8 (access: 10.05.2014). Plans to build a new Berlin Brandenburg International Airport (BER) are also relevant for Polish ports. The primary and necessary condition for BER to become a big interchange is assigning to BER the role of the hub by one of the global European carriers, however the only air carrier to be considered would be Lufthansa.

[136] Polish airports operate as limited companies: limited liability companies (7 regional airports: GDN, KTW, KRK, LCJ, POZ, RZE, SZZ) and joint-stock companies (2 regional airports: BZG and WRO). Two airports (WAW and IEG) are state enterprises.

[137] Particularly noteworthy is the role of the PPL, which currently manages the WAW airport and IEG regional airport, and owns shares in other ports, transformed in 1990s into commercial companies (with the exception of LCJ regional airport).

torical circumstances), but also take into account the development potential. Structured basic internal sources, affecting the competitive position that can be referred to the airport, are shown in Table 8.

Table 8. Basic internal sources of airport competitiveness

Types of sources	Source characteristics
Legal basis	**Competitiveness of an airport resulting from legal norms** regulated legal status of land ownership (e.g. lease agreement), ownership structure
Size and the specificity of natural resources	**Competitiveness of an airport based on the location and area of the land owned** total airport area, environmental conditions and the resulting restrictions on the use of the airport, limited capacity, *limited use area* for the particular airport, map of airport obstacles, airport operational parameters, etc.
Basic infrastructural facilities	**Competitiveness of an airport resulting from the available infrastructural facilities** facilities available with appropriate parameters to enable smooth functioning of airport runways, taxiways, aircraft parking planes, terminals, cargo buildings, hangars, car parks etc. Also water-supply system, power network and related equipment including energy-saving devices to reduce the costs
Communication system	**Competitiveness of an airport resulting from the available internal communication** efficient internal communication system in the port area, terminal with connections to other modes of transportation (bus and rail stations, special walkways) tunnels linking the port with the communication system of the region, expressway exit on the highway, connections with urban centres through rail, railcars, connection to the main roads, motorways (necessity to build roundabouts, exits, tunnels)
Facilities for a high level of safety	**Competitiveness of an airport resulting from IT systems and equipment** the equipment of the airport for radar navigation ILS, NDB, DVOR, the equipment for Airport Rescue and Fire Service (fire station buildings, fire engines), equipment and resources of the airport for adverse conditions in the winter (ploughs and equipment for clearing runways)
Capital resources	**Competitiveness of an airport resulting from capital resources** financial capital resources, ability to raise capital (e.g. issuance of bonds), structure of revenues and expenses, etc.
Human resources	**Competitiveness of an airport resulting from human resources** level of education and professional qualifications, training opportunities, organizational structure of the port, etc.

Quality policy	**Competitiveness of an airport resulting from the adjustment to quality improvement requirements** ensuring high level of services provided (e.g. assuring high quality services for persons with disabilities), the introduction of high standards of quality (ISO), participation in programs, quality testing, etc.
Marketing management	**Competitiveness of an airport resulting from better assessment of market needs** conducting broad and attractive marketing activities (e.g. directed to carriers – a system of fees and discounts targeted at passengers – loyalty programs), attention to the logo and the brand of the port, carrying out marketing research, etc.
Executive management	**Competitiveness of an airport resulting from managerial skills** management expertise, managerial talent, and the resultant introduction of innovative activities, etc.
The vision and mission of the airport and further development plans	**Competitiveness of an airport resulting from the vision and mission** defined plans based on developed vision and mission of the port, general plans, master plans and the resulting planned and on-going investments in the port area

Source: own study.

Within the group of internal determinants, issues of skilful management of the airport, efficient investment policy, as well as implementation of a suitable policy for safety, quality and marketing, deserve special attention. Marketing activities provide a way to distinguish the airport among its competitors, especially by building a strong airport brand.

Managers, responsible for the growth of airports and for the policy of the enterprise they manage, should have the ability to assess the benefits and the scale of risk pertaining to developing airport services in the region. They should also possess adequate knowledge on the use of analytical tools for the analysis of demand and reduction of investment risks, as well as a practical approach to methods of increasing the efficiency of airport marketing. The managerial competencies of the Management Board of the airport include cooperation with key stakeholders, i.e. individual clients (passengers) and institutional clients (airlines), but also with local and State government units in the region. In the case of a regional airport, managers may also use the experience of international experts in designing cooperation between the airport and other entities (region or carriers).

5. COMPETITIVENESS MODEL OF A REGIONAL AIRPORT

In this chapter of the monograph, the authors distinguish the most important factors pertaining to the competitiveness of Polish regional airports (in terms of passenger transport). A devised econometric model is presented, which enables assessment of the significance and the impact of individual features taken from the already established dataset (potential regressors) on shaping the competitive position of individual Polish regional airports.

Based on the availability of feature measurements, the empirical material consisted of data from 11 Polish regional airports in the years 2007–2010 (the present study includes only those airports, which were actually operating in the analysed period). The above-mentioned data is panel-type data, and simultaneously comprises the features applicable to cross-sectional data and time-series data. This is due to the fact that they have been established as a result of observation of identical objects in subsequent time periods. In this particular case, 11 objects referred to 11 airports ($n = 11$), whose features were subjected to observation in four subsequent years ($T = 4$). The total count of nT sample was 44 object-periods. The advantage of panel data is that it provides a greater amount of information about these objects. Panel data enables simultaneous consideration of the diversity of studied objects, and observation of their evolution in time.

One of the measures of the share of a given airport in the total share of passenger transport is the percentage of the number of passengers served by the given airport to the total number of passengers served by all airports considered within the analysed group. The random variable, which describes market shares, or fractions (designated respectively on the basis of analysis), assumes values in the range of <0, 1>. We should add that the sum of values assumed by this feature for individual units, observed in the same period, equals 1.

Considering the above, the model applied to the relationship between dependent variable, which describes the summed fractions and the explanatory variables, needs to include the specific character of the former variable. In the case of cross-sectional data, one of the possible applications is the so-called multinomial fractional logit, with parameters estimated as quasi-MLE (quasi-Maximum Likelihood Estimator).[138] However it should be noted that the number of objects-airports (11) is too small to devise an assessment model for cross-sectional data. Because the inferring procedure in quasi-MLE models employs an asymptotic covariant estimator matrix, its carry out procedure based on such a scarce sample would generate very uncertain results.

One of the alternatives could feature the application of panel data, data pertaining to 11 Polish regional airports, during four subsequent years. Nevertheless, in this particular situation, fractional logit model would require the application of a unique estimation procedure, including panel data.

With regard to the aforementioned assumptions, the authors decided to assume the dependent variable in a wholly different format. This particular variable would not possess a limited interval of variability, and in consequence, this would enable the application of linear models for panel data. Among basic linear models to be used for panel data we can distinguish a fixed effects model and a random effects model.[139] These models differ in terms of the method of considering individual effects and their association with the operation of factors, which are constant in time.

In consequence, the dependent feature has been selected, and this particular measure has a theoretically unlimited variability range, which enabled the assessment and comparison of competitive position of Polish regional airports. Specifically this measure is referred to as the coefficient of the number of passengers served by Polish regional airports, per 100 residents of the given region, in which the given airport was situated (pax/100 residents). Quite a favourable property, which results from the structure of the aforementioned indicator, is the fact that it expresses the magnitude of passenger traffic in terms of the potential catchment area. It should be noted at this point that the catchment area was determined in a simplified manner according to data availability pertaining to the number of inhabitants in a given voivodship. This particular indicator is not merely an exclusive measure of the magnitude of passenger traffic but it can be regarded as a measure of the competitive position of the airport (it informs us about the level of usage of the potential catchment area by the airport).

---

[138] More information about this particular model and information regarding the methods of estimating its parameters can be found in: L.E. Papke, J.M. Wooldridge, "Econometric Methods for Fractional Response Variables with an Application to 401(k) Plan Participation Rates," *Journal of Applied Econometrics* 11(6), 1996.

[139] Detailed description of the most frequently applied linear models for panel data (fixed effects, random effects and the dynamic Arellano-Bond model) can be found in the following papers: W.H. Greene, *Econometric Analysis. Sixth Edition*, Pearson, Prentice Hall 2008; B.H. Baltagi, *Econometric Analysis of Panel Data*, John Wiley & Sons, 2001; C. Hsiao, "Analysis of Panel Data," Cambridge University Press, 2003.

The dataset of potential explanatory features includes variables in the form of indicators. This results from the fact that this particular form of dependent variable has been selected. This simply means that variables were generated by transforming the features, whose values had been gathered from data repositories, such as the Local Data Bank of the Central Statistical Office of Poland and from the Civil Aviation Bureau database.

Limited access to current data pertaining to Polish regional airports was one of the significant restrictions in determining the set of potential variables, which explain the analysed model. In reality, the data was available for only few years back. In the selection process, the authors paid particular attention so that the variables included in the potential regressor model would pertain to a variety of factors within the groups. This was discussed in detail in chapter four, where the specific taxonomy was presented.

In the beginning of the chapter, a brief description of linear models and their application to panel data is discussed. It should be pointed out that they are theoretically applied in econometric analysis. Subsequently, definition of variables is presented (including potential model regressors) and a preliminary empirical analysis is performed. Next, the specification and estimation of the econometric model is described. This model demonstrates conditioning factors pertaining to pax/100 inhabitants indicator for 11 Polish airports (2007–2010). The chapter ends with conclusions and a brief summary, which pertains to the empirical determinants of the competitive position of Polish regional airports within the aviation market.

5.1. Linear econometric models for panel data – a brief theoretical description

The structure of the analysed data considered herein is presented in the form of balanced panel data with the following dimensions. In practice, this means that features of all 11 objects (airports) are observed in each of the 4 time periods, specifically in the years 2007–2010. In the case of unbalanced panel data,[140] the number of periods in which observations were performed varies considerably.

In the case of a larger number of studied objects , and a small number of observation periods , the properties associated with non-stationary character,[141] which comprises a time series panel, should not be substantially exhibited. Hence in this particular case, based on the approach widely used in

---

[140] Adoption of unbalanced panel is linked with the application of a different analytical approach.

[141] Such as for example: possibility to obtain apparent regressions, in the case of operating on not-transformed non-stationary series, which express the feature level, as opposed to working with a varied series in order to obtain stationarity.

scientific literature, data series observed in such a short time range are considered stationary within this range. Therefore, when constructing this type of model, we operate in terms of these features and not based on variables generated by the differentiation of primary features.

The next step in model specification is to determine the types of individual effects, that is, to qualify them as either fixed or random. This selection is usually based on empirical premises, however in some cases there exist theoretical circumstances that support the application of a given model. With regard to empirical premises, in the case where individual effects are correlated with explanatory model features, the parameter estimator for random effects model ceases to be compatible. This fact is associated with the construction of the random effects model:

$$y_{it} = x_{it}'\beta + (\alpha + u_i) + \varepsilon_{it}, \ (i = 1, ..., n, \ t = 1, ..., T)$$

in which individual effects for objects ($i = 1, ..., n$) are included by the introduction of non-observable random variable u_i, the values of which are independent of time t.

Therefore in the case where there exists a correlation between variable u_i and variables which explain the model $E(u_i | X_i) \neq 0$, this leads to the violation of one of the principles of the theorem pertaining to generalized linear regression model, and in consequence GLS (Generalized Least Squares)[142] estimator ceases to be a compatible estimator for the parameters which pertain to the random effects model.

The result of the Hausmann test[143] and the compatibility of the (F)GLS (Feasible Generalized Least Squares) estimator constitute principal empirical premises, which are decisive in selecting between the random effects model and the fixed effects model. Nevertheless, there are situations, in which the selection of the model type, based exclusively on the result of the aforementioned test, are not that evident.

A more detailed description of the random effects model including the procedures for its estimation (employing generalized Least Squares Method) is presented in the work of Green.[144] At this point we will briefly describe the fixed effects model.

---

[142] Generalized version of least squares method.

[143] Hausmann test is based on the fact that in the case of a correlation between explanatory variables and the random component (in this particular situation random variable describes individual effects) the RE estimator ceases to be a compatible estimator for model parameters with fixed effects. Nevertheless in the case of a lack of such a correlation this estimator is compatible and becomes the most efficient in linear class.

[144] W.H. Greene, *Econometric Analysis*, op. cit.

The construction of fixed effects model permits the existence of correlations between explanatory variables X_i and individual effects c_i. Derived from general model, we have the following terms:

$$y_{it} = x_{it}'\beta + c_i + \xi_{it}, (i = 1, ..., n, t = 1, ..., T)$$

where $E(c_i | X_i) = h(X_i)$.

Due to the fact that the conditional expected value $E(c_i | X_i)$ for individual effect for i-th object is identical for each of considered periods t, the aforementioned general model can be expressed as:

$$y_{it} = x_{it}'\beta + h(X_i) + \xi_{it} + [c_i - h(X_i)] = x_{it}'\beta + \alpha_i + \xi_{it} + [c_i - h(X_i)].$$

Hence parameter α_i, explicitly included in the model, bears a portion of individual effects, which result from their correlation with explanatory variables: $E(c_i | X_i) = h(X_i) = \alpha_i$, whilst non-observable component $[c_i - h(X_i)]$ is no longer correlated with explanatory features. For the designation of the sum $\xi_{it} + [c_i - h(X_i)]$ we employ component ε_{it}, and subsequently obtain the following form of the fixed effects model:

$$y_{it} = x_{it}'\beta + \alpha_i + \varepsilon_{it}, (i = 1, ..., n, t = 1, ..., T),$$

where:
y_{it} is the explaining variable for i-th object in t period,
α_i is the distinct parameter for each i-th object, constant in time for non-variable model; due to the fact that differentiation between the objects is included by assuming a distinct α_i parameter for each object, which is constant in time (and not by introducing a non-observable variable u_i to the model, that would describe individual effects), the aforementioned model is referred to as the fixed effects model,
x_{it} is the vector which explains features for i-th object in t-time,
ε_{it} is the random component for i-th object in t-time.

If the assumptions are satisfied regarding the sphericity[145] of the vector ε, which includes random components ε_{it}, then in order to estimate the parameters for fixed effects model we need to employ the Least Squares Dummy Variable method (LSDV), which is equivalent to the application of LS (Least Squares) model estimation method. Beside the explanatory variables

---

[145] Random vector has a multidimensional normal distribution with the following set of parameters: $E(\varepsilon) = 0$ and $S^2(\varepsilon) = E(\varepsilon\varepsilon') = \sigma^2 I$; equivalent with this term: $\varepsilon \sim N(0, \sigma^2 I)$.

gathered in the matrix we have to attach 0–1 type variables, which form the $\mathbf{D} = [D_1\, D_2\, ...\, D_n]$ matrix,[146] and subsequently we obtain the ultimate expanded matrix for explanatory features in the form $\mathbf{Z} = [\mathbf{X}\,|\,\mathbf{D}]$.

Matrix $\mathbf{Z}$ can also be presented in the block form, which emphasizes the panel type data:

$$\mathbf{Z} = \begin{bmatrix} \mathbf{Z}_1 \\ \mathbf{Z}_2 \\ \vdots \\ \mathbf{Z}_n \end{bmatrix} = \begin{bmatrix} \mathbf{X}_1 & \mathbf{D}_1 \\ \mathbf{X}_2 & \mathbf{D}_2 \\ \vdots & \vdots \\ \mathbf{X}_n & \mathbf{D}_n \end{bmatrix}$$

, where $\mathbf{Z}_i$ block includes observations for i-th object in subsequent time periods.

Also y vector pertaining to the explanatory value for objects i ($i = 1, ..., n$) observed in subsequent time periods ($t = 1, ..., T$) can be expressed in block form:

$$\mathbf{y} = \begin{bmatrix} \mathbf{y}_1 \\ \mathbf{y}_2 \\ \vdots \\ \mathbf{y}_n \end{bmatrix}$$

, where block y_i includes observations for i-th object in subsequent time periods.

Vector which estimates parameters based on the LSDV method is expressed in the following form:

$$\hat{\boldsymbol{\beta}}_{LSDV} = \begin{bmatrix} \hat{\boldsymbol{\beta}}_{LSDV} \\ \hat{\boldsymbol{\alpha}}_{LSDV} \end{bmatrix} = (\mathbf{Z}'\mathbf{Z})^{-1}\mathbf{Z}'\mathbf{y} = \left(\sum_{i=1}^{n} \mathbf{Z_i}'\mathbf{Z_i} \right)^{-1} \left(\sum_{i=1}^{n} \mathbf{Z_i}'\mathbf{y_i} \right)$$

, where $\hat{\boldsymbol{\alpha}}$ is the parameter estimation vector which corresponds to 0-1 variables (these parameters describe the impact of individual effects), and $\hat{\boldsymbol{\beta}}$ is the parameter estimation vector for explanatory features.

More formal and detailed description of the procedure for estimating the parameters of fixed effects model, which employs LSDV method, can be found in the aforementioned work by Green.

In the case where random vector sphericity ε is absent,[147] the LSDV estimator remains compatible with the parameters of the fixed effects model, however it ceases to be the most efficient linear estimator (BLUE). One

---

[146] Number of 0–1 variables is equal to the number of objects observed in subsequent time periods. 0–1 variable D_i ($i = 1, ..., n$) assumes value 1 in case of i-th object and value 0 in remaining cases.

[147] $S^2(\varepsilon) = E(\varepsilon\varepsilon') = \Omega = \sigma^2\Phi,\ \Phi \neq I.$

of the possible deviations from sphericity is the occurrence of the so-called groupwise heteroskedasticity. In the case of the occurrence of groupwise heteroskedasticity, random components ε_{it} which comprise the random vector ε and correspond to the objects that belong to the same i-th group, are characterized by the same level of variance, which is different from the level of variance in objects which belong to other groups. Therefore each i-th group of objects possesses its own unique level of variance, which corresponds to random components ε_{it}.

In this particular situation, the covariant matrix for random vector[148]

$$\varepsilon = \begin{bmatrix} \varepsilon_1 \\ \hline \varepsilon_2 \\ \hline \vdots \\ \hline \varepsilon_n \end{bmatrix}$$

assumes the following block-diagonal form:[149]

$$S^2(\varepsilon) = E(\varepsilon\varepsilon') = \Omega = \begin{bmatrix} \sigma_1^2 I_T & 0 & \cdots & 0 \\ 0 & \sigma_2^2 I_T & \cdots & 0 \\ \vdots & \vdots & \ddots & \vdots \\ 0 & 0 & \cdots & \sigma_n^2 I_T \end{bmatrix}.$$

For panel data, these types of groups can generate observations, which pertain to the same i-th object in subsequent time periods ($t = 1, ..., T$).

Hence blocks ε_i ($i = 1, ..., n$) for vector ε rank group of components correspond to observations of i-th object in subsequent time periods ($t = 1, ..., T$), and subsequent diagonal blocks of covariant vector matrix ε correspond to covariant matrices for individual $S^2(\varepsilon_i) = \sigma_i^2 I_T$ objects.

In the case of the occurrence of random vector groupwise heteroskedasticity for panel data, the best unbiased linear estimator (BLUE) pertaining to the parameters of fixed effects model appears to be the LSDV estimator (WLS[150]):

$$\hat{\beta}_{WMNK} = \begin{bmatrix} \hat{\beta}_{WMNK} \\ \hat{a}_{WMNK} \end{bmatrix} = (Z'\Omega^{-1}Z)^{-1} Z'\Omega^{-1}y = \left(\sum_{i=1}^{n} \left(\frac{1}{\sigma_i^2}\right) Z_i'Z_i\right)^{-1} \left(\sum_{i=1}^{n} \left(\frac{1}{\sigma_i^2}\right) Z_i'y_i\right).$$

---

[148] In vector ε Block ε_i groups random components which correspond to objects that belong to the i-th group ($I = 1, .., n$).

[149] For the sake of simplicity, equal count T has been assumed for all groups.

[150] Weighted Least Squares method.

WLS (Weighted Least Squares) estimator assumes comprehension of matrix, however in practice, its form is unknown. Therefore it is necessary to estimate its elements and this particular approach is referred to as the Least Squares Method – (F)WLS.[151]

To conclude our description of the model estimation procedure, it seems appropriate to mention theoretical (factual) premises, which are decisive in selecting one of the two principal types of models for panel data.

In reference to theoretical premises, which are decisive in choosing between the fixed effects model and the random effects model, the following are assumed:

- fixed effects model (FE) is applied to cases where the data set comprises all objects, which belong to the population, and which are observed in subsequent periods, while the estimates of parameter α_i enable comparisons of individual differences between every single object considered in the analysis;
- random effects model (RE) is applied where the dataset comprises a sample of objects that have been matched to a larger population, for which an observation is performed in subsequent time periods; in this case the distribution of individual effects is described by the non-observable variable, corresponding to the individual effects of objects that were included in the sample and also the ones that have not been included.

5.2. Definition of variables and their preliminary analysis

This subchapter describes the definitions that have been employed in subsequent statistical analysis of variables. Also, it features a preliminary empirical analysis. Firstly empirical analysis is conducted which pertains to the conditioning factors of the pax/100 inhabitants coefficient calculated for individual Polish regional airports in the years 2007–2010. It should be noted that this coefficient was treated as the dependent variable in the model. They are presented in depth in the annex (see: Group A.1. *Box plot for a dependent variable* – pp. 151). Next, the definitions pertaining to potential variables that explain the model have been discussed as well as empirical analysis has been performed based on the panel data gathered.

The preliminary empirical analysis of features was commenced starting from the coefficient, which served the role of Y dependent variable in the constructed model. Table 9 presents the basic statistical description for variable Y, the arithmetic mean, the total variance as well as the share of total

---

[151] Feasible Weighted Least Squares method.

variability pertaining to the intergroup variance feature (for panel data, it is more appropriate to refer to "inter-object" variance).[152] In addition, standard deviation and coefficient of variation have been calculated (designated based on the total variance).

Table 9. Descriptive statistics for variable Y: number of passengers served by the airport per 100 inhabitants of the region in which the airport is situated

Variable	N Signifi-cant	Mean	SD Standard Deviation	Coeffi-cient of variation	Inter-group variance	Internal variance
Y (pax/100 inhab.)	44	49.32	48.67	98.69%	99.00%	1.00%

Source: own study.

In order to assess the significance of diversity of mean levels pertaining to the coefficient of the number of passengers served by the airport per 100 inhabitants (2007–2010), the ANOVA variance analysis has been employed.

Within the confines of ANOVA analysis, we have to verify the null hypothesis, which assumes that average values of the considered coefficient in the given time period were equal for individual objects; this is stated in the null hypothesis test:

$$H_0 : \mu_{i^*} = \mu_{j^*}$$

$$H_1 : \exists i, j : \mu_{i^*} \neq \mu_{j^*}, i, j = 1, 2, ..., 11; i \neq j$$

Below, in table 10 the results of ANOVA and Leven's tests are presented. The Leven's test verifies the homogeneity of variance in groups (that is the absence of diversity of the coefficient of variation in the years 2007–2010 among individual airports.

Despite the fact that the ANOVA test assumes the existence of intergroup variance homogeneity (in this case we are dealing with homogeneity of the feature's variance in time, for each of the analysed objects), this test is resistant to a violation of this assumption.[153] As Leven's test results indicate (p-value at 0.0055 level), significant diversity has been noted for individual Polish airports.

---

[152] Also in: E. Grabińska, *Determinanty konkurencyjności regionalnego portu lotniczego*, Uniwersytet Jagielloński, Kraków 2014 (PhD Thesis), quote, annex, p. 284.

[153] Discussion pertaining to this subject can be found in: *Elektroniczny podręcznik statystyki*, StatSoft 2006.

Table 10. ANOVA test for variable Y

		ANOVA test analysis Effects in bold are significant with p < 0.05000						
Variable	SS effect	df effect	MS effect	SS Error	df Error	MS Error	F	p
pax/100 inhab.	100857.7	10	10085.77	1019.463	33	30.893	326.476	5.25E-30
		Leven's Test homogenous variance Effects in bold are significant with p < .05000						
Variable	SS effect	df effect	MS effect	SS Error	Df SS Error	MS SS Error	F	p
pax/100 inhab.	236.940	10	23.694	243.632	33	7.383	3.209	0.0055

Source: own study.

Graph 1. Number of passengers per 100 inhabitants of the region in the years 2007–2010 based on individual airports

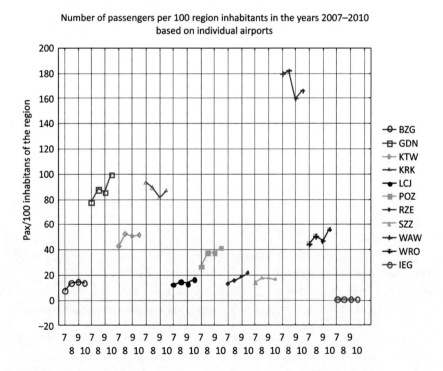

Source: own study.

According to our assumptions, despite the violation of the principles pertaining to variance homogeneity (taking into account the resistance of ANO-VA test), we shall attempt to interpret the results.

The ANOVA test indicates the occurrence of diversity between average levels of the pax/100 inhabitants coefficient for individual Polish airports. The high statistical significance of these differences is reflected in the very low level of p value (p-value = 5.25e – 30). In addition, a very important analysis pertains to values of (p-value = 5.25e – 30). Graph 1. presents the time series of the pax/100 inhabitants coefficient for 11 Polish airports.[154]

Detailed analysis of Graph 1 indicates a generally increasing trend of the studied coefficient for the majority of Polish regional airports.

Definition of potential explanatory variables of the model and their preliminary empirical analysis

A set of potential explanatory variables comprised 16 features. Presented below is a list of indicators calculated on the basis of features selected as a result of compromise. The values for the 11 Polish airports for 2007–2010 are taken from the aforementioned data repositories (Table 11).

Table 11. Potential explanatory variables for the constructed model, including their abbreviated meaning

t	temporal variable
X1	the number of routes served by the airport (symbol: routes_served)
X2	the number of carriers serving the airport (symbol: carriers)
X3	passenger fee amount for domestic traffic in the airport in PLN (symbol: fees_domestic)
X4	passenger fee amount for international traffic in the airport in PLN (symbol: fees_intl)
X5	mean passenger fee amount in the airport in PLN (symbol: fees_avg)
X6	the percentage of operations carried out by low-cost carriers as a share of total operations performed in the airport (symbol: lowcost_op [%])
X7	the percentage of operations carried out by charter carriers as a share of total operations performed in the airport [%] (symbol: charter_op [%])
X8	the percentage of operations carried out by traditional carriers in all operations performed in the airport [%] (symbol: trad_op [%])
X9	the percentage of domestic operations in all operations performed in the airport [%] (symbol: fees_domestic [%])

---

[154] In order to maintain clarity for x axis on the graph, the following designations have been assumed 7, ..., 10 for 2007, ..., 2010.

t	temporal variable
X10	the percentage of international operations in all operations performed in the airport [%] (symbol: fees_intl [%])
X11	GDP per capita in the region (voivodship), where the airport is situated in thousand PLN per capita (symbol: GDP PC [thous. PLN/inhab.])
X12	the number of workers employed in the R&D sector per 10 thousand inhabitants (symbol: R&D employees/10 thous. inhab.)
X13	number of tourists visiting the region, in which the airport is situated, per 100 residents of this region (symbol: tourists [pers./100 inhab.])
X14	the number of kilometers of public roads per 100 km² region (symbol: roads [km/100 km² of the area])
X15	the number of kilometers of railway lines per 100 km² region (symbol: rail [km/100 km² of the area])

Source: own study.

Below are the basic descriptive statistics for the aforementioned characteristics, such as the arithmetic mean, standard deviation, coefficient of variation and the share in the total features' variance of the intergroup ("inter-object") and intercompany ("temporal") variance.

In addition, ANOVA test results are presented (empirical value of F and the corresponding p-value) assuming, in the null hypothesis, the equality of average values of the properties for all objects (Table 12).

For each variable, we rejected the hypothesis of equality of the mean value for all objects, while the share of intergroup variance ("inter-facility") in the total variance remained at the level of 71.7% (X3 – fees_domestic) to 99.9% (X15 – railways).

The high share of intergroup ("inter-facility") variance, which testifies to a high differentiation in the mean values of time-dependent characteristics, and potential explanatory characteristics for the test objects, seems to suggest that typical individual effects exist for particular objects.

The charts, which include the panel data characteristics, enable the assessment of conditioning of potential explanatory features. They are presented in depth in the annex (Group A.2. *Box plots for potential explanatory features of the model* [graphs II–XVIII] – pp. 151–158) and (Group B. *The box plot compiling dependent model variables including potential regressors [scatter charts: pax /100 inhabitants indicator in regard to individual potential explanatory features [graphs XVIII–XXXII] – pp. 159–166).*[155]

---

[155] See also: E. Grabińska, *Determinanty konkurencyjności...*, op. cit., annex, pp. 284–292, 292–299.

Table 12. Principal descriptive statistics for potential explanatory features of the model and results of F test for ANOVA model

Variable	N significant	Mean	Standard deviation	Coefficient of variation	Intergroup variance	Internal variance	F (ANOVA)	p (ANOVA)
X1	44	70.59	59.43	84.19%	96.01%	3.99%	79.39	3.8E – 20
X2	44	43.23	34.40	79.58%	94.91%	5.09%	61.57	2.0E – 18
X3	44	25.52	8.24	32.28%	71.69%	28.31%	8.36	1.4E – 06
X4	44	33.92	13.37	39.40%	99.85%	0.15%	2219.01	0.0E + 00
X5	44	29.72	9.49	31.94%	95.35%	4.65%	67.62	4.7E – 19
X6	44	35.26	17.72	50.26%	87.21%	12.79%	22.49	5.9E – 12
X7	44	6.84	5.06	73.93%	78.84%	21.16%	12.29	1.7E – 08
X8	44	57.90	21.38	36.92%	85.11%	14.89%	18.86	6.6E – 11
X9	44	34.90	24.65	70.63%	90.18%	9.82%	30.31	8.6E – 14
X10	44	65.10	24.65	37.87%	90.18%	9.82%	30.31	8.6E – 14
X11	44	33.76	8.11	24.03%	90.88%	9.12%	32.88	2.6E – 14
X12	44	29.22	14.51	49.66%	98.91%	1.09%	299.30	2.2E – 29
X13	44	12.16	7.89	64.90%	98.17%	1.83%	176.58	1.1E – 25
X14	44	131.83	36.95	28.03%	99.20%	0.80%	410.77	0.0E + 00
X15	44	7.55	3.34	44.22%	99.94%	0.06%	5104.56	0.0E + 00

Source: own study.

5.3. Developing the model for the "pax per 100 inhabitants" coefficient and identifying the features, which significantly influence the level of that coefficient

Given the fact that the empirical material formed a panel comprising 11 Polish airports (whose characteristics were observed in the subsequent years 2007–2010), that means all these airports were active in the examined time period, hence they were considered as population and selected for the description of existing dependencies in the model with fixed effects (fixed effects FE).

The next section of the chapter presents the assumed procedure that results in the construction of a model, for which the significance of impact of individual regressors on explaining variability of dependent feature has been verified. Explanatory variables of the accepted model created the dataset (based on empirical circumstances), which has a significant impact on the pax/100 inhabitants coefficient for Polish airports in the years 2007–2010.

The analysis of the dataset, as well as the selection and assessment of the model was performed using the *gretl* model.[156] Next, after analysing the force and direction of the dependence between individual pairs of features, the specification of the model with established effects has been presented.

Due to the fact that the 3 features: the share of traditional operations, the share of domestic operations, and the average passenger fee are accessible, we are able to designate the linear combination of other features from the dataset of potential model regressors with fixed effects. This is achieved in the following manner: as a combination of 0–1 variables with, respectively: in the first case, the share of low-cost operation and charter operations, in the second case, the share of international operations, and in the last case, as combination of two features only: the amount of passenger fee in domestic traffic and the amount of passenger fee in international traffic. After applying the aforementioned conditions, these redundant values are rejected from the set of potential explanatory features. The next phase of the analysis includes the set of potential model regressors, which comprise 13 features.

The starting point in the procedure of model specification with fixed effects was to assume the main criterion of model selection among $2^m - 1 = 2^{13} - 1 = 8190$ alternatives.[157] As the principal model selection criterion we have assumed Akaike minimal values of informative index (AIC). This particular index, in its basic version, is defined as the sum multiplied by -2 logarithmic likelihood function l and the double number of p model parameters:

$$AIC = -2l + 2p.$$

The form (logarithm) of the likelihood function depends on the construction of the model as well as the form of distribution of random vector model. In the case of LSDV estimator for fixed effects model with multidimensional distribution of normal random vector, which fulfills the sphericity condition, logarithm likelihood function and AIC criterion data are expressed as follows:

$$l = \ln L = -\frac{nT}{2}\left(1 + \ln 2\pi - \ln nT\right) - \frac{nT}{2}\ln \sum_{i=1}^{n}\sum_{t=1}^{T} e_{it}^2 \quad (LSDV)$$

---

[156] http://www.kufel.torun.pl (access: 10.04.2014).

[157] 2^m refers to the number of subsets for potential regressors, where m is the number of potential explanatory features.

$$AIC = -2l + 2p = nT\left(1 + \ln 2\pi - \ln nT\right) + nT \ln \sum_{i=1}^{n} \sum_{t=1}^{T} e_{it}^{2} \; _{(LSDV)} + 2p$$

where

$e_{it\;(LSDV)}$ is the remainder of the model with parameters that were estimated by LSDV method for i-th object in t-time.

Because it was not possible to know the form of distribution of the random vector in advance, we have assumed its sphericity, which imposed the assumption of the aforementioned form (logarithm) of likelihood function. The set of potential models has been confined to a few, which were distinguished by the lowest level of AIC criterion based on the assumed likelihood function. Consequently a couple of candidate-models have been established, which were submitted to further verification.

One of the most significant steps in the assessment of candidate-models was the verification of the assumption pertaining to the distribution of random vector.

LSDV standard errors (for candidate-models) pertaining to the estimation of parameters, have been derived on the basis of the covariant estimator matrix, which subsequently was designated by employing the sphericity assumption of the random vector distribution.[158] The aforementioned errors substantially differed from the ones that have been derived on the basis of resistant estimation of covariant estimator matrix.[159] This particular fact means that the assumption pertaining to the sphericity of the random vector distribution is not fulfilled. As a result, the LSDV estimator remains compatible, but at the same time it ceases to be the most effective estimator to describe the parameters of the linear model with fixed effects. Additionally, the assumed form of the likelihood function (simultaneously the AIC criterion) does not reflect the regularities, which can be found in the distribution of the random vector models, and in this form, the AIC criterion appears to be invalid for the selection of the optimal model.

In order to determine the linear estimator, which would be more efficient than the LSDV estimator, it is necessary to establish the type of deviations that exist between the multi-dimensional distribution of the random vector and the spherical vector.

---

[158] $S^2\left(\hat{\beta}_{LSDV}\right) = \sum_{i=1}^{n} \sigma_i^2 \left(Z_i'Z_i\right)^{-1}.$

[159] $S_{robust}^2\left(\hat{\beta}_{LSDV}\right) = \left(Z'Z\right)^{-1} Z'\Omega Z\left(Z'Z\right)^{-1}$, where estimation of matrix components Ω assumes that: $\sigma_{it,jr} \approx e_{it}e_{jr}$, where $i, j = 1, ..., n; t, r = 1, ..., T.$

Results of tests conducted for candidate-models were in favour of the occurrence of the groupwise heteroskedasticity in the random vector distribution. Therefore the random components, which corresponded to individual objects, were characterized by a different level of variance (constant in time).

In a similar manner, in order to select the optimal model (in the sense of including groupwise heteroskedasticity), it is necessary to assume a different form of the likelihood function as well as AIC criterion. In the case of the occurrence of groupwise heteroskedasticity, the likelihood function logarithm and the AIC criterion are presented as follows:

$$l = \ln L = -\frac{nT}{2} \ln 2\pi - \frac{T}{2} \sum_{i=1}^{n} \ln \hat{\sigma}_i^2 - \frac{1}{2} \sum_{i=1}^{n} \frac{\sum_{t=1}^{T} e_{it}^2}{\hat{\sigma}_i^2}$$

$$AIC = -2l + 2p = nT \ln 2\pi + T \sum_{i=1}^{n} \ln \hat{\sigma}_i^2 + \sum_{i=1}^{n} \frac{\sum_{t=1}^{T} e_{it}^2}{\hat{\sigma}_i^2} + 2p$$

where e_{it}^2 is the remainder of the i-th object in t-period for the (F)WLS estimated model,
$\hat{\sigma}_i^2$ is an estimation (non-variable in time) of the variance of the random component for the i-th object.

(F)WLS estimator for parameters pertaining to fixed effects model, which includes the existence of groupwise heteroskedasticity, is expressed by the following equation:

$$\hat{\beta}_{EWMNK} = \begin{bmatrix} \hat{\beta}_{EWMNK} \\ \hat{\alpha}_{EWMNK} \end{bmatrix} = \left[\sum_{i=1}^{n} \left(\frac{1}{\hat{\sigma}_i^2} \right) \mathbf{Z_i'Z_i} \right]^{-1} \left[\sum_{i=1}^{n} \left(\frac{1}{\hat{\sigma}_i^2} \right) \mathbf{Z_i'y_i} \right]$$

$$\hat{\sigma}_i^2 = \frac{\mathbf{e_{i\ (KMNK)}'e_{i\ (KMNK)}}}{T}$$

where
$\mathbf{e}_{i\ (LSD)V} = \begin{vmatrix} e_{i1\ (LSD)V} & \cdots & e_{iT\ (LSD)V} \end{vmatrix}'$ $(i = 1, ..., n)$ – is the residual vector for i-th object, which pertains to the model with estimates for LSDV parameters.

Based on the findings, the procedure regarding the search for the optimal model with minimal level of AIC information criterion was repeated. To estimate the parameters of the model, (F)WLS has been applied, and the optimal selection was conducted on the basis of the minimal level AIC criterion, which in this particular case included groupwise heteroskedasticity. Further analysis was performed according to the (F)WLS parameter estimations model, which was characterized by the lowest AIC level (additionally, a few supplementary models have were considered). The information criteria for the selected model turned out to be lower than the ones obtained for reserve models, and subsequently the values were adopted, which are shown in Table 13.[160]

Table 13. Information criteria for selected model estimated by (F)WLS

Likelihood logarithm	−60.1484	Akaike criterion (AIC)	152.2967
Schwarz criterion (SC)	180.8438	Hannan-Quinn criterion (HQ)	162.8834

Source: own study.

The occurrence of groupwise heteroskedasticity for the selected model is confirmed by the test, which assumes homoskedasticity of the random component variance in the null hypothesis (Table 14).

Table 14. Results of the statistical test for groupwise heteroskedasticity

Chi-square (11) = 626.255	p = 3.3769e − 127	Panel residual variance = 9.47102

Source: own study.

Table 15. Variance of dependent variable (pax/100 inhabitants) in time according to units

unit (i)	variance
1.	8.70466 (T = 4)
2.	14.305 (T = 4)
3.	3.13662 (T = 4)
4.	12.8409 (T = 4)
5.	14.6947 (T = 4)
6.	10.6022 (T = 4)
7.	1.02829 (T = 4)
8.	8.34139 (T = 4)
9.	14.7432 (T = 4)
10.	14.8793 (T = 4)
11.	0.90501 (T = 4)

Source: own study.

---

[160] Due to their non-standardized character, the values of information criteria are compared with competing models. The lower the value of information criteria (AIC, BIC), the more preferable the model.

Low p-value equal to 3.4e – 127 favours the rejection of the null hypothesis.

The derived model with fixed individual effects, which describes the conditioning of the pax/100 inhabitants coefficient (that includes 5 regressor features – 4 features with values variable in time, and a linear trend) assumes the following form:

$$y_{it} = \hat{\alpha}_i + \hat{\beta}_1 t + \hat{\beta}_2 \cdot x_{1,it} + \hat{\beta}_3 \cdot x_{6,it} + \hat{\beta}_4 \cdot x_{11,it} + \hat{\beta}_5 \cdot x_{12,it} + e_{it}$$

where

Dependent Variable:

Y *pax_100_inhab*$_{it}$ – value of the coefficient which pertains to the number of passengers served per 100 inhabitants of the given region for i-th airport in t-year.

Model Explanatory Variables:

t – linear deterministic trend ($t = 1, ..., 4$),

X1 (*routes_served*$_{it}$) – number of routes served by for i-th airport in t-year

X6 *lowcost_op*$_{it}$ – percentage of operations performed by low-cost carriers in i-th airport in t-year (%),

X11 (*GDP_PC*$_{it}$) – region's GDP registered in the t-year, in which the i-th airport is located (thous. PLN/inhab.),

X12 (*R&D_employees*$_{it}$) – coefficient pertaining to the number of people employed in Research and Development (employees/10 thousand inhab.).

Estimations of α_i parameters, which describe individual effects:

$\hat{\alpha}_1$ – BZG (Bydgoszcz airport),

$\hat{\alpha}_2$ – GDN (Gdańsk airport),

$\hat{\alpha}_3$ – KTW (Katowice airport),

$\hat{\alpha}_4$ – KRK (Kraków airport),

$\hat{\alpha}_5$ – LCJ (Łódź airport),

$\hat{\alpha}_6$ – POZ (Poznań airport),

$\hat{\alpha}_7$ – RZE (Rzeszów airport),

$\hat{\alpha}_8$ – SZZ (Szczecin airport),

$\hat{\alpha}_9$ – WAW (Warsaw airport),

$\hat{\alpha}_{10}$ – WRO (Wrocław airport),

$\hat{\alpha}_{11}$ – IEG (Zielona Góra airport),

e_{it} – remainder component for i-th airport in t-time.

Estimations of model parameters along with results pertaining to significance tests for given parameters, as well as diagnostic statistics for this model, are presented in three subsequent Tables: 16, 17 and 18.[161]

---

[161] By D_i, i = 1,...,11 0–1 variables have been designated, which enable the inclusion of individual effects characteristic for individual airports in the fixed effects model.

Table 16. (F)WLS estimation model with 44 observations

11 cross-sectional units have been included
Dependent variable Y: pax_100_inhab.

	Coeffi-cient	Standard error	T-student test	P value	Signifi-cance
t	2.7167	1.2522	2.1695	0.0387	**
routes_served (X1)	0.3335	0.0624	5.3417	0.0000	***
lowcost_op_% (X6)	0.2099	0.0888	2.3635	0.0253	**
PC_GDP (X11)	−1.7351	0.7606	−2.2812	0.0303	**
R&D_employees (X12)	1.0042	0.3173	3.1646	0.0037	***
BZG AIRPORT (D1)	23.3121	20.0414	1.1632	0.2546	
GDN AIRPORT (D2)	74.3697	22.1192	3.3622	0.0023	***
KTW AIRPORT (D3)	46.7561	24.3725	1.9184	0.0653	*
KRK AIRPORT (D4)	34.7939	21.4144	1.6248	0.1154	
LCJ AIRPORT (D5)	−8.6900	21.4493	−0.4051	0.6885	
POZ AIRPORT (D6)	22.3296	24.7558	0.9020	0.3748	
RZE AIRPORT (D7)	20.8886	15.3966	1.3567	0.1857	
SZZ AIRPORT (D8)	26.8350	19.8467	1.3521	0.1872	
WAW AIRPORT (D9)	122.3170	37.8614	3.2307	0.0032	***
WRO AIRPORT (D10)	52.9400	25.3024	2.0923	0.0456	**
IEG AIRPORT (D11)	33.0613	19.1862	1.7232	0.0959	*

Significance: p-value < 0.1 *, < 0.05 **, < 0.01 ***
Source: own study.

Table 17. Principal statistics for weighed data

Sum of Residual Squares	39.6595	Residual standard error	1.1901
R-square Det. Coeff.	0.9967	Adjusted R-square	0.9950
F(15, 28)	572.2633	Value p for F test	1.68e-30
Likelihood Logarithm	60.1484	Akaike informative criterion	152.2967
Bayes-Schwarz Criterion	180.8438	Hannan-Quinn criterion	162.8834

Source: own study.

Table 18. Principal statistics for original data

Arithmetic mean for dependent variable	49.3193	Standard Deviation for dependent variable	48.6748
Sum of Residual Squares	430.4062	Residual standard error	3.9207

Test for differentiation of free expression in groups – null hypothesis: groups possess common free expression *test statistics: F(10, 28) = 95.2855, value p 6.55e – 019*

Source: own study.

Prior to performing an interpretation of the parameters' assessment for the devised model, we have to carefully examine the values of diagnostic statistics, and conduct combined and individual assessments of the significant impact of the features, which were included in the model. The aforementioned assessments are performed in order to properly evaluate the model selection. The results of these analyses will have a decisive impact on accepting or rejecting the model.

We should keep in mind that the principal diagnostic statistics for this model (residual standard error, R^2, F *test*) in the case of applying the (F)WLS estimator are designated on the basis of weighed data.

The starting point will feature a method for designating residual, regressive and total sum of squares for weighed data, based on which the diagnostic measures have been obtained in the case of using the (F)WLS estimator (groupwise heteroskedasticity).

Error Sum of Squares (SSE) is expressed as follows:

$$SSE = \sum_{I=1}^{N} \left(\frac{1}{\hat{\sigma}_i^2} \right) \mathbf{e_i}'\mathbf{e_i} = 39,6595$$

where

$\mathbf{e_i} = \mathbf{y_i} - \hat{\mathbf{y}}_i$ – residual value vector (F)WLS for i-th object (airport)

where

$\mathbf{y_i} = [y_{i1} \, ... \, y_{iT}]'$ – dependent variable vector (pax/100 inhabitants) for i-th object (airport) in subsequent years ($t = 1, ..., T$);

$\mathbf{Z_i} = [\mathbf{z_{i1}} \, ... \, \mathbf{z_{iT}}]'$ – (expanded in terms of values which enable the identification of the i-th object) value matrix for explanatory features of the i-th object in subsequent years ($t = 1, ..., T$);

whilst $\mathbf{z}_{it} = [d_{1it} \, ... \, d_{iit} \, ... \, d_{nit} \, x_{1it} \, ... \, x_{Kit}']$ and d_{jit} are values which identify i-th object,

such that, $d_{jit} = \begin{cases} 0, & \text{gdy } j \neq i \\ 1, & \text{gdy } j = i \end{cases}$, $j = 1, ..., n$, a is a number which represents

explanatory model features;

$\hat{\boldsymbol{\beta}}_{EWMNK} = \begin{bmatrix} \hat{\alpha}_1 & ... & \hat{\alpha}_n & \hat{\beta}_1 & ... & \hat{\beta}_K \end{bmatrix}'$ – (F)WLS estimation of parameters for fixed effect model;

$\hat{\mathbf{y}}_i = [\hat{y}_{i1} \, ... \, \hat{y}_{iT}]' = \mathbf{Z_i}\hat{\boldsymbol{\beta}}_{EWMNK}$ – theoretical values vector (model type) for i-th object (airport) in subsequent years ($t = 1, ..., T$).

Weighed squares sum total () is expressed by the following formula:

$$SST = \sum_{I=1}^{N} \left(\frac{1}{\hat{\sigma}_i^2} \right) \mathbf{y_i}'\mathbf{y_i} - nT\bar{y}^2 = 39,6595$$

where

$$\bar{y} = \frac{1}{nT} \sum_{i=1}^{n} 1' \left(\frac{1}{\hat{\sigma}_i} \right) \mathbf{y_i}$$ – weighed arithmetic mean for dependent variable

represents a vector with dimension $Tx\ 1$ which is comprised entirely of the values of one.

Weighed regressive square sums (SSR) is given as follows: $SSR = SST - SSE$. Residual standard error (weighed) is devised in the following way:

$$s_e = \left[\frac{SSE}{nT - n - K} \right]^{\frac{1}{2}} = \left[\frac{39,6595}{28} \right]^{\frac{1}{2}} = 1,1901.$$

Determinant coefficient R^2 informs us about what percentage of variance pertaining to the dependent variable is explained by the model.

R^2 is a standardized measure which assumes values within the range $\langle 0, 1 \rangle$, and in case of using the (F)WLS estimator, based on the weighed data calculated from the following equation:

$$R^2 = 1 - \frac{SSE}{SST}$$

Using the model constructed in this manner, we are able to explain 99% of the variance in the dependent variable. This means that the model selection to weighed empirical data is well matched.

The value of the adjusted R^2 coefficient (designated by the symbol $\bar{R}^2$) is used to compare the adjustments of "competing" models, with different sets of explanatory features. This comparison is conducted because it includes both the level of the projection of empirical data by the model, and its level of complexity. The construction of the $\bar{R}^2$ coefficient impacts the fact, that with an unchanged level of explanatory feature of the dependent variable, the preferred model is the one with the lowest number of parameters, for which this particular coefficient is larger.

Adjusted $\bar{R}^2$ coefficient is given by the following formula:

$$\bar{R}^2 = 1 - \frac{nT - 1}{nT - n - K} \frac{SSE}{SST}$$

$\bar{R}^2$ coefficient, in the model with individual fixed effects, can assume values in the range $\left\langle \frac{1 - n - K}{nT - n - K}, 1 \right\rangle$

For the considered model, $\bar{R}^2$ coefficient has assumed the value equal to 0.9950. This value was greater than values obtained for competing (alternative) models.

F test for which hypotheses are posed as follows:[162]

$$H_0 : \alpha_1 = \alpha_2 = ... = \alpha_n = \mu_{\bullet\bullet} \quad \text{and} \quad \beta_1 = \beta_2 = ... = \beta_K = 0$$

$$H_1 : \exists i : \alpha_i \neq \mu_{\bullet\bullet} \quad \text{or} \quad \exists k : \beta_k \neq 0$$

enables us to assess the combined significance of the impact on the dependent variable (pax/100 inhabitants coefficient), of explanatory features with values that are variable in time, as well as individual effects, which comprise the impact of features that are constant in time.

F test statistics are given as follows:[163]

$$F_{emp} = \frac{SSR}{SSE} \cdot \frac{nT - n - K}{n + K}$$ and in the case of authenticity of the null hypothesis,

it has the F-Snedecor type distribution with degrees of freedom as given: $v_1 = n + K$ and $v_2 = nT - n - K$

The empirical value of the F test for the considered model corresponded to value p equal to 1.68e – 30. The very low value of p justifies rejection of the null hypothesis in favour of an alternative hypothesis, which acknowledges the existence of linear dependence between the pax/100 inhabitants coefficient for Polish airports and the 5 devised explanatory features (variable in time) as well as the individual effects that reflect the impact of factors, which are constant in time.

For non-weighed data, the standard residual error for the constructed model equals 3.92 passengers/100 inhabitants.

Based on the aforementioned diagnostic analysis, we have ultimately approved the selected model as a tool, which describes the dependence between the coefficient of the number of passengers served by an airport per 100 inhabitants of the region, and the model's regressors, while considering individual effects.

Values observed for pax/100 inhabitants as well as theoretical values, designated according to the fixed effects model which has been assumed, were collected and revised in the annex (Group C. *Table listing the observed values of the for pax/100 inhabitants coefficient, and theoretical values, designated on the basis of fixed effects model for 11 Polish airports in the years 2007–2010 –* pp. 167–168).

---

[162] $\mu_{\bullet\bullet}$ is the unconditional mean value for the dependent variable, in this case, pax/100 inhabitants.

[163] SSE and SSR are designated according to weighed data.

The most crucial impact on the conditioning of the level of modelled coefficient for Polish airports in the years 2007–2010, taking into account p value which corresponds to t test results pertaining to the parameters' significance, is exhibited by the following features: the number of routes served by airports and the number of R&D employees per 10 thousand inhabitants of the region (p – $value$ < 0.01). Subsequent features are the following: percentage of low-cost carrier operations, per capita GDP in the region served by the airport, and deterministic linear trend ($0.01 \leq p$ – $value$ < 0,05).

As it turned out, in the case of Polish airports, a very significant role was played by interactions of individual effects. The impact of the latter was included by simply introducing them into the parameters model α_i ($i = 1, ..., 11$), different for each airport.

The power of the impact of individual effects for given airports on the pax/100 inhabitants coefficient can be examined by employing the F test. This particular test verifies the hypothesis about the equality of parameters α_i ($i = 1, ..., 11$), the purpose of which is to include in the model the impact of factors, constant in time, which are characteristic for each airport.

The null hypothesis for F test assumes that α_i parameters for all of the objects – airports ($i = 1, ..., 11$) are equal, whilst the alternative hypothesis states that there exists a pair of parameters: α_i and α_j which have different values.

Test hypotheses can be formally written as follows:

$$H_0 : \alpha_i = \alpha_j$$
$$H_1 : \exists i, j : \alpha_i \neq \alpha_j \qquad (i, j = 1,...,11; i \neq j).$$

If the null hypothesis is true, the statistical data for F-Snedecor distribution is: $v_1 = n - 1 = 10$ with $v_2 = nT - n - K = 10 = 44 - 11 - 5 = 28$ degrees of freedom.

The empirical value of the F test equals 95.2, which corresponds to the p-value at the 6.55e-019 level. The result of the test clearly justifies rejection of the null hypothesis. It should be noted that this hypothesis assumes lack of differences in terms of the level of parameters, which describe the impact of individual effects on the level of the modelled coefficient.

The impact of individual effects on the level of pax/100 inhabitants coefficient (the resultant of invariable factors present in the studied time period, 2007–2010, which are not directly included in the model) is expressed by estimating the values of $\hat{\alpha}_i$ parameters for individual airports.

The impact of individual effects in the studied period increases the modelled value of the pax/100 inhabitants coefficient for individual Polish airports. This increase results only from the impact of features with variable values by subsequent values, and it is as follows (ranked in descending order):

- WAW: 122.3 passengers/100 inhabitants of the region,
- GDN: 74.4 passengers/100 inhabitants of the region,
- WRO: 52.9 passengers/100 inhabitants of the region,
- KTW: 46.8 passengers/100 inhabitants of the region,
- KRK: 34.8 passengers/100 inhabitants of the region,
- IEG: 33.1 passengers/100 inhabitants of the region,
- SZZ: 26.8 passengers/100 inhabitants of the region,
- BZG: 23.3 passengers/100 inhabitants of the region,
- POZ: 22.3 passengers/100 inhabitants of the region,
- RZE: 20.9 passengers/100 inhabitants of the region.

Only in the case of LCJ, the $\hat{\alpha}_5$ parameter estimation, which describes the impact of individual effect for that airport, assumed a negative value (−8.7). This fact reflects the combined negative impact of invariable factors (in time) on conditioning the modelled coefficient for Łódź airport.

At this point we attempt to present our interpretation of the estimated model parameters, which go hand in hand with variables that change their value over time.

A positive deterministic trend has been observed for the pax/100 inhabitants coefficient, which has been included in the model as the t variable. This fact confirms the existence of independent increments in terms of the value of coefficient for all Polish airports in subsequent years (2007–2010). These increments are on average 2.7 passengers served per 100 inhabitants of the region.

With regard to the number of routes served by the Polish airports, their unit growth has resulted in the growth of the modelled coefficient by 0.33 passengers per 100 inhabitants of the region. It should be emphasized that the levels of other features have remained unchanged. Meanwhile the increase in the share of low-cost carriers' operations in the total number of operations has increased by 1 per cent, *ceteris paribus*, for Polish airports it was reflected by an increase of 0.22 passengers per 100 inhabitants of the region.

In the years 2007–2010, per capita GDP for Polish airports serving a given region (voivodship) has increased by 1000 PLN/inhabitant. This means, *ceteris paribus*, that it corresponded to the decrease of the modelled coefficient by 1.7 passengers per 100 inhabitants of the region. At first glance, the negative value of this particular parameter appears to be rather surprising, nevertheless considering the analysed time period, we can assume that the decrease in the level of economic activity in the regions (measured by regional per capita GDP) could lead to the increase in the number of foreign paid-work migrations. In this particular case, aircraft was selected as the first choice of travel, and this was reflected in the increase of the coefficient pertaining to the number of passengers served per 100 inhabitants of the region.

The unitary increase in the coefficient pertaining to the number of workers employed in the research and development sector (in a given region) per 10 thousand inhabitants, is reflected *ceteris paribus,* in the increase of pax/100 inhabitants coefficient by exactly 1.00 passenger per 100 inhabitants of the region.

In the final section, the substantive interpretation of results obtained from econometric analysis will be presented.

5.4. Study results and a brief summary of competitive position determinants

For 11 Polish airports in the studied time period 2007–2010, among the factors influencing the competitive position on the passenger transport market, as measured by the index of the number of passengers per 100 people in the region (pax/100 inhabitants), 4 features have been observed, which exhibited time variability. In addition, independent deterministic upward trend was observed as well as a significant impact of factors (constant in time) has been noted in the form of individual effects for given airports.

We should point out however, that the empirical analysis was limited to devising factors that condition the competitive position in only one dimension, which in this case was their position on the air transport market. Therefore we need to remember that the purpose of this analysis was not to devise factors, which comprehensively shape the competitive position of the airport.

Factors, which have been taken into account in this particular model, have been based on empirical premises. Subsequently they can be treated as determinants of the competitive position for individual Polish airports in the passenger transport market in the years 2007–2010.

The following factors were singled out, which exhibited growth in the studied time period, at the same time reflecting the increased competitive position of Polish airports, expressed in the pax/100 inhabitants coefficient:

- number of routes served by an airport – increased number of destinations, which can be accessed through the airport enhances its competitive position (high statistical significance of impact);
- R&D activities in the region served by an airport – measured by the number of employees of R&D sector per 10 thousand inhabitants of the region, seems to be the indication of the scientific and technological level of the region served by a given airport; the higher that level is, the larger the demand for air travel, which directly corresponds to higher level of the indicator pertaining to the number of passengers served by airports with extensive science and technological supply base (WAW and KRK airports);

- Percentage of low-cost carrier operations in the total number of airport operations – due to more extensive accessibility, the increasing share of low-cost carrier operations in a given airport is associated with lower prices. This fact directly translates to the increase of the coefficient pertaining to the number of passengers served per 100 inhabitants.

Another interesting observation in the studied time period (2007–2010) was the increase in the number of passengers served by airports, which seems surprising when we take into account the fact that in general, economic growth has slowed down in that period. This fact can be explained by the increasing number of paid-work travel, mainly served by air transport. This is clearly reflected in the increase of the pax/100 inhabitants coefficient.

The crucial factors, which determine the competitive position of individual Polish airports in terms of air transportation, are the indices, which are constant in time, whose impact is reflected in the individual effects, characteristic for particular airports in Poland. Due to the fact that construction of the fixed effects model does not provide opportunities to include only those features with constant values for individual airports (through the analysis of the impact of individual effects), we are entitled to pose only hypotheses in terms of their sources. This is compounded by the fact that different sets of factors are considered for different airports.

Consequently the highest positive impact of individual effects on shaping the coefficient of the number of passengers served was observed for Warsaw Airport. We can speculate that this strong positive effect was associated with the presence of time-constant factors such as: the role of Warsaw airport as the central airport and a regional hub, as well as the administrative role of the Polish capital. Among regional airports, high positive impact of individual effects (although considerably lower than in the case of Warsaw) was observed for Gdańsk and Wrocław airports. We can speculate that the high positive impact in the case of the aforementioned airports was associated with the absence of other airports (within 100 km), which would offer an extensive network of routes served.

The lowest values of parameters, which describe the impact of individual effects was registered for Łódź airport (negative value) and Rzeszów airport. In particular, the negative impact on the level of pax/100 inhabitants coefficient (Łódź airport) can be possibly linked to the existence of the central Warsaw airport, which is located closer than 100 km. In this particular case, passengers are fully aware of this proximity and prefer to use the central airport. In the case of Rzeszów, the low parameter may be associated with the peripheral character of this airport and the presence of a much larger (and more popular) Kraków airport.

Summing up, we should reiterate that empirical analysis was limited to distinguishing factors, which condition exclusively only one of the dimensions of competitive position. In this case, it was the measured coefficient pertaining to the number of passengers served by an airport per 100 inhabitants of the region in which that airport is located.

Due to the fact that the character of certain dimensions of competitive position is difficult to measure, the establishment of factors, which shape competitive position requires a different methodological approach, and the application of other sources of data. In order to establish significant factors, which shape the competitive position (in multi-dimensional aspect), we employ data obtained from expert type surveys. Such data has been transformed and evaluated by employing quantitative methods appropriate for this type of data (i.e. fuzzy logic, AHP).[164]

---

[164] Example of this type of procedure carried out in order to distinguish the most important factors of multi-dimensional competitive position can be found in the following works: J.H. Huang, "Fuzzy Rasch Model in TOPSIS: A New Approach for Generating Fuzzy Numbers to Assess the Competitiveness of the Tourism Industries in Asian Countries," *Tourism Management* 33, 2012; G.I. Crouch, "Modelling Destination Competitiveness: a Survey and Analysis of the Impact of Competitiveness Attributes," *CRC for Sustainable Tourism*, 2007.

CONCLUSIONS

Over the past years, the Polish civil aviation sector – regional airports in particular – has been developing intensively. As a consequence of the political transformation of the 1990s and Poland's accession to the European Union, there were strong institutional and legal changes. Socio-economic conditions, in which both old and new Polish airports operate, have changed significantly as well. Transformation that has occurred in the last two decades in Poland and in Europe contributed to the increased competition in the air transport market.

The phenomenon of competition is generally seen as a positive economic category influencing the growth of business efficiency, and favouring the restoration of equilibrium in the economy. However, in times of crisis, intensification of competitiveness can make it difficult for entities, operating in the demanding and difficult air services market, to function and generate income. It may even threaten their existence. Therefore, management boards of companies are looking for reliable and objective data – information and measures of competitiveness – to make accurate business decisions.

In the case of airports (compared with enterprises in the classical meaning of the word), the situation is far more complex, because a modern airport is a very sophisticated economic organism, the functioning of which is not so easy to evaluate. The progressive processes of globalization and liberalization, as well as the associated internationalization of air transport, contribute to the enhancement of competitiveness in this sector. These processes also apply to Polish airports, which had been transformed into objects of a new type. Their main and essential purpose is to increase the efficiency of management and to improve competitiveness. The problem of the development of air transport, and the associated issue of the competitive position of the airport, is relatively well presented in foreign literature. However, in Polish literature it has not been shown in enough depth. This monograph has designated and specified determinants of competitiveness of Polish regional airports, which are necessary for the strategic management of the airports. The field of strategic competitiveness was shown by multilateral relationships and dependencies between a regional airport and various external determinants, and by relating them to actions by the managers of the regional airport. The conditions and changes in the development of Polish regional airports in the period from 2007 to 2010 were taken into account, and the possibilities and limitations associated with their further, efficient operation in the air services market were presented, especially in the segment of passenger services. The success of airports in the highly competitive conditions consists of many related components, which affect their competitive position in the air transport market. On the basis of a list of potential factors, which shape competitiveness of the regional airport operating in the Polish market, an econometric analysis of associations between their sets was conducted, in order to determine the major growth factors of competitiveness of all 11 airports operating in Poland.[165] In the econometric model, which has been created for the purpose of this study, the dependent variable was the ratio of the number of passengers served by the airport, per 100 inhabitants of the region (voivodship) where the port is located. The construction of the measure enabled an assessment of the competitive position of the regional airport with respect to the approximate sphere of influence (*catchment area*) of that airport.[166]

The scope of quantitative analysis was limited by the temporal availability of data for Polish airports. This prevented an evaluation of the long-term impact of macroeconomic factors on the competitiveness of Polish ports (in particular those related to business cycles). Thus, a set of potential explanatory variables of the model was formulated, using features (factors) from the micro- and meso-environment of the Polish airports.

Among the features of factors at the macro-environment level, the following possible regressors of the constructed model were taken into account:

- number of routes served by the airport,
- level of airport charges (international and national),
- share of low cost and charter operations, as well as the sum of all operations in the given airport.

As far as meso-environment is concerned, among others, the following variables were taken into consideration:

- measures of socio-economic development of the region served by the airport:

---

[165] In the period considered, the point structure of civil aviation in Poland consisted of: 1 central port (PL WAW) and 11 regional airports (BZG, GDN, IEG, KRK, KTW, LCJ, POZ, RZE, SZZ, WRO). The Mazury Szczytno-Szymany Airport (SZY) has halted its business activities, therefore the airport was not taken into account in the study.

[166] Considering the availability of data on the population of voivodships, for simplicity's sake it's assumed that the catchment area of the port is the entire voivodship in which the airport is located.

- – GDP per capita for the voivodship in which the seat of the airport is located;
- – number of people employed in the aviation sector, per 100 inhabitants of the region;
- – number of kilometres of roads, as well as kilometres of railroad per 100 km² of the voivodship's area;
- measure of tourist attractiveness of the regions served by the given airport:
  - – number of tourists per 100 inhabitants of the region in which the airport is located.

The data used in the analysis constituted the panel data, so it was possible to examine the significance of the impact of individual factors, stable over time, characteristic for particular Polish airports. The study took into account 11 objects, as this was the number of Polish airports operating during the studied period. Thus, the objects were 11 airports ($n = 11$), the characteristics of which were subjected to observation in 4 consecutive years, from 2007 to 2010 ($T = 4$). Therefore, the total sample size nT was 44 object-periods.

The results of econometric analysis demonstrated that individual effects of the airport (which are stable over time and specific to particular airports), play the main part in elucidating the volatility of the ratio (of the number of passengers per 100 inhabitants of the region), which measures the competitiveness of Polish airports. In short, the conclusion that may be drawn is that the impact of the individual effects on the competitiveness of the ports is due to their characteristic features, which are stable over time, and among these unmeasured factors one may indicate:

- historically established position of airports – the dominant role of the central port and ports in major cities and regional agglomerations (among others, in Kraków – KRK, Katowice – KTW, Gdańsk – GDN or Wrocław – WRO)

and

- location and proximity to a given airport in relation to another airport – the distance between an analysed airport and the nearest competitor airport (the impact of this element became apparent especially in the case of the airport in Łódź, for which a strong negative nature of the individual effect was observed; LCJ seems to be behind in the air services market race against the nearby central airport – Warsaw Chopin Airport (formerly Warsaw-Okęcie Airport) – WAW).

The econometric analysis also demonstrated that among those examined characteristics, which were variable in time, the following factors profoundly shaped the degree of competitiveness of particular Polish airports from the micro-environment level (determining the relationship between ports and airlines):

- number of routes served by the airport;

and

- share of low-cost carriers' operations in the total number of operations in that airport.

The latter factor, shaping the competitiveness of ports and measured by the number of passengers per 100 inhabitants, is strongly associated (during the survey period) with high levels of economic migrations of Poles to Western European countries, whose journeys were serviced mainly by low cost carriers.

Among the relevant factors, which are subjected to the change in time, we can distinguish the following from a set of regional environmental factors (meso-environment) of Polish airports (considered as a possible model regressors):

- GDP per capita for the region

and

- the number of employees working in R&D sector per 10,000 inhabitants of the region, in which the airport is located.

The first variable can be regarded as an approximate measure of socio-economic growth of the region served by the port, and the second indicator becomes an approximate measure of the level of scientific and technological progress. An increasing trend of the ratio of the number of passengers per 100 inhabitants of the region was observed for all the ports. It is essential to remember that, in the analysis, this ratio was adopted as a measure of the level of competitiveness.

It should be emphasized that the conclusions of the econometric analysis refer only to the period under examination (the end of the first decade of the 21st century), so they are not prospective in nature. Due to the relatively short period of time, the scope of systematically collected quantitative data, concerning the activity of Polish airports, is limited – therefore, this unfortunately hinders any in-depth empirical analysis of their competitiveness in a more breadth and in longer term. However, the aforementioned econometric model of regional airport competitiveness upgrades and extends analytical perspective, therefore it can be used as an instrument supporting executive decisions in the management of the currently operating airports. It may also form the basis for rational planning of new regional airports.

The performed analysis makes it possible to formulate the conclusion that the competitive position of Polish regional airports depends on the strength of the home region – the state of its socio-economic growth, its potential, and development prospects.

Determinants of the home region, as well as infrastructure and technological facilities of the port, remain burdened with historical baggage – and therefore, it is relatively difficult to move on with new challenges and accomplish more within a short period of time, despite substantial investments. It should also be noted that although the origins of Polish aviation go back to the 1920s, historical conditions (the destruction caused by World War II and economic backwardness of the communist era) meant that only in the last two decades, Polish regional airports began to play a greater role in the national economy.

Polish regional airports are becoming highly relevant, and their market share is growing steadily. It is expected that in the coming years, Polish regional airports will continue to develop – to increase their capacity and market share, and most of the operations to be carried out just to/from regional airports.[167]

According to experts, Polish geopolitical location – in the centre of Europe, between East and West – is strategically excellent for the development of this sector of the economy. Polish regional airports already joined the Central European transit network and became more attractive partners for many entities. Although in comparison with the market of our neighbours (e.g. Germany) Polish passenger traffic continues to grow at a fairly slow pace,[168] it should be noted that limitations and exhaustion of airport capacity located in countries of the so-called old European Union, mean tremendous prospects for Polish airports. As a result of such optimistic forecasts for the next decade, investments in Polish airport infrastructure are envisaged. New possibilities and scenarios of development, which are opening for airports in general, may

---

[167] On the one hand, Polish regional airports are to handle approx. 56% of all air operations. It is forecasted that KRK, KTW, GDN, WRO and POZ airports will record strong development, particularly in the case of European but also intercontinental connections. They will gain approx. 170% of passengers (in the pessimistic scenario) to 340% (in the optimistic scenario) and their combined market share will amount to 47–51%. On the other hand, the market share of RZE, SZZ and BZG airports will rise from the current 4% to 9% of total Polish market in 2035. Source: *Prognoza rozwoju transportu lotniczego w Polsce. Raport cząstkowy 2*, 22 March 2010. Prepared on behalf of the Ministry of Infrastructure by the Gesellschaft für MKmetric System planung, http://siskom.waw.pl/komunikacja/lotnisko/CPL/analiza_2010/cpl_analiza_2010_raport_czastkowy_2.pdf (access: 10.12.2014), p. 70.

[168] For example, in 2010, the number of passengers served by all Polish airports amounted only to 20 million passengers. For comparison, in the same year the two biggest German airports recorded passenger traffic at Frankfurt (FRA) – 53 million pax, Munich (MUC) – 34 million pax.

also be available to Polish regional airports. Above all, airports should ensure safe take-offs and landings of aircrafts and efficient passenger handling. However, as already indicated, an airport is becoming a new type of facility, called the *Airport City* – the economic entities are not only earning profits, but they also act as a magnet, attracting other companies and becoming catalysts for regional development. Therefore, the regional airports are treated as multi-modal nodes of strategic importance for the regions.[169] A region-building role of the regional airport translates into strengthening the competitive position of the home region of the airport, on the other hand, the strong competitive position of the home region of the port determines effective development of the regional airport. Therefore, airport managers should seek the support of regional authorities, hence the role of the local and regional authorities in strengthening the competitive position of the port deserves special attention.

The current, very high dynamics of the air transport market development may be added to the relational dynamics of regional airports. Therefore, the competitiveness of Polish regional airports, presented in this study, should not be seen as a photograph, but rather as a movie – a picture remaining in constant motion. We hope that each reader should find in this research work some information or discussion on the strategic management of airports, which shall prove useful to him or her for professional or personal reasons.

---

[169] It should be emphasized that Polish labour market surveys conducted by the Civil Aviation Office in Poland suggest that in the next 10–15 years the demand for people with expertise in the field of civil aviation will increase. On the basis of the presented perspective of air traffic, it can be estimated that in the coming years the aviation-related areas will employ more than 100 thousand new employees.

LIST OF TABLES AND FIGURES, DRAWINGS AND GRAPHS

List of tables

List of figures

List of drawings

LITERATURE

Legal acts

European legal acts

1. Komunikat Komisji, *Wytyczne Wspólnotowe dotyczące finansowania portów lotniczych i pomocy państwa na rozpoczęcie działalności dla przedsiębiorstw lotniczych oferujących przeloty z regionalnych portów lotniczych*, Dz.Urz. UE nr 2005/C 312/01, 9.12.2005.
2. Organizacja Międzynarodowego Lotnictwa Cywilnego, *Polityki ICAO dotyczące opłat dla portów lotniczych i służb żeglugi powietrznej, zatwierdzone przez Radę i opublikowane jej decyzją*, dok. 9082, 8th edition, 2009, http://www.ulc.gov.pl/_download/regulacja_rynku/oplaty_lotniskowe/icaopl0209.pdf.
3. Rozporządzenie Komisji (WE) nr 1828/2006 z dnia 11 lipca 2006 r. ustanawiające szczegółowe zasady wykonania rozporządzenia Rady (WE) nr 1083/2006 ustanawiającego przepisy ogólne dotyczące Europejskiego Funduszu Rozwoju Regionalnego, Europejskiego Funduszu Społecznego oraz Funduszu Spójności oraz rozporządzenia (WE) nr 1080/2006 Parlamentu Europejskiego i Rady w sprawie Europejskiego Funduszu Rozwoju Regionalnego. Dz.Urz. UE, L 371/1, 27.12.2006.
4. Rozporządzenie nr 300/2008 Parlamentu Europejskiego i Rady z dnia 11 marca 2008 r. w sprawie wspólnych zasad w dziedzinie ochrony lotnictwa cywilnego i uchylającego rozporządzenie (WE) 2320/2002 oraz przepisów wykonawczych do tego rozporządzenia, Dz.Urz. UE, L 97/73, 9.04.2008.
5. Rozporządzenie Rady (EWG) nr 95/93 z dnia 18 stycznia 1993 r. w sprawie wspólnych zasad przydzielania czasu na start lub lądowanie w portach lotniczych Wspólnoty, Dz.Urz. UE, L 14, 22.01.1993.
6. Umowa o Wspólnym Obszarze Lotniczym między Unią Europejską i jej państwami członkowskimi a republiką Mołdawii, Dz.Urz. UE, L 292/3, 20.10.2012.

Polish legal acts

1. Konwencja o międzynarodowym lotnictwie cywilnym, podpisana w Chicago 7 grudnia 1944 r., Dz.U. z 1959 r., nr 35, poz. 212.
2. Rozporządzenie Ministra Infrastruktury z dnia 14 kwietnia 2004 r. w sprawie opłat lotniskowych dla państwowych statków powietrznych wykonujących loty związane z zapewnieniem bezpieczeństwa publicznego, bezpieczeństwa państwa, ochroną granicy państwowej lub poszukiwaniem i ratownictwem, Dz.U. z 2004 r., nr 122, poz. 1268.
3. Rozporządzenie Ministra Infrastruktury z dnia 29 kwietnia 2004 r. w sprawie opłat lotniskowych, Dz.U. z 2004 r., nr 103, poz. 1083.
4. Rozporządzenie Ministra Infrastruktury z dnia 30 kwietnia 2004 r. w sprawie klasyfikacji lotnisk i rejestru lotnisk cywilnych, Dz.U. z 2004 r., nr 122, poz. 1273.
5. Rozporządzenie Ministra Infrastruktury z dnia 25 maja 2009 r. w sprawie obsługi naziemnej w portach lotniczych, Dz.U. z 2009 r., nr 83, poz. 695.
6. Ustawa z dnia 31 maja 1962 r. – Prawo lotnicze, ogłoszona w Dz.U. PRL Nr 32, poz. 153 z dnia 8 czerwca 1962 r.
7. Ustawa z dnia 23 października 1987 r. o przedsiębiorstwie państwowym "Porty Lotnicze," Dz.U. z 1987 r., nr 33, poz. 185.
8. Ustawa z dnia 3 lipca 2002 r. – Prawo lotnicze, Dz.U. z 2002 r., nr 130, poz. 1112.

Strategic documents, reports and analysis

1. ACI, *Air Quality Directive Compliance. Survey at European Airports*, December 2003, http://www.airports.org.
2. ACI, *Building for the Future – Paying for the Airports of Tomorrow*, April 2005, http://www.airports.org.
3. ACI, *The Social and Economic Impact of Airports*, January 2004, http://www.airports.org.
4. ACI, *Understanding Airport Business*, 2006, http://www.airports.org.
5. ACI, *World Airport Traffic Report 2010*, http://www.airports.org.
6. Air Transport Research Society, *Airport Benchmarking Report – Global Standards for Airport Excellence*, Part I, II, III, Vancouver 2002.
7. ATAG, *Aviation Benefits Beyonds Borders*, March 2012, http://www.aviationbenefits beyondborders.org/download-abbb-report.
8. ATAG, *The Economic & Social Benefits of Air Transport*, Geneva, September 2005.
9. *Biała księga. Plan utworzenia jednolitego europejskiego obszaru transportu – dążenie do osiągnięcia konkurencyjnego i zasoboszczędnego systemu transportu*, Bruksela 2011, dated 28.3.2011 KOM(2011), 144 final version, KE.
10. Boeing, *Current Market Outlook 2012–2031*, http://www.boeing.com/commercial/cmo/ pdf/Boeing_Current_Market_Outlook_2012.pdf.

11. European Commission, *Impact Assessment of the Single Aviation Market on employment and working conditions for the period 1997-2007*, Brussels 2010, http://ec.europa.eu/transport/modes/air/internal_market/doc/sec_2010_503_en.pdf.

12. Eurostat, *Civil Aerospace in the 21 Century, Price Waterhouse Coopers*, January 2006, http://epp.eurostat.ec.europa.eu/statistics_explained/index.php/Passenger_transport_statistics.

13. Komisja Wspólnot Europejskich, *Europejska polityka transportowa 2010: czas na podjęcie decyzji*, COM (92) 494 final, Bruksela, 2.12.1992, http://aei.pitt.edu/1116/1 /future_transport_policy_wp_COM_92_494.pdf.

14. Komisja Wspólnot Europejskich, *Europejska polityka transportowa w horyzoncie do 2001 r.: czas wyborów*, COM (2001) 370, Bruksela, 12.09.2001, http://www.polloco.pl/ pdf/biala_ksiega_pl.pdf.

15. Liwiński, J., *Działalność portów lotniczych na świecie w 2009 r.*, ULC, Warszawa 2010.

16. Liwiński, J., *Działalność portów lotniczych na świecie w 2011 r.*, ULC, Warszawa 2011.

17. Ministerstwo Infrastruktury, *Informacja o kierunkach rozwoju lotnictwa cywilnego do roku 2010*, Warszawa 2003.

18. Ministerstwo Infrastruktury, *Koncepcja Lotniska Centralnego dla Polski – prace analityczne. Raport cząstkowy 1: Analiza obecnego stanu (lata 2000–2008) rynku transportu lotniczego w Polsce na tle rynku europejskiego i światowego*, 31st January 2010 r., p. 27, http://www.transport.gov.pl/file/0/1794291/czastkowy1.pdf.

19. Ministerstwo Infrastruktury, *Polityka transportowa państwa na lata 2006–2025*, Warszawa 2005,https://www.google.pl/?gws_rd=ssl#q=Polityka+transportowa+pa%C5%84stwa+na+lata+2006%E2%80%932025%2C+Warszawa+.

20. Ministerstwo Infrastruktury, *Projekt Strategii Rozwoju Transportu na lata 2007–2013*, Warszawa 2004.

21. Ministerstwo Infrastruktury, *Słowniczek pojęć transportowych SRT*, załącznik 3 do *Strategii Rozwoju Transportu*, Warszawa, 30th March 2011, http://www.transport. gov.pl/files/0/1793934/Za03SRTSowniktransportowySRT.pdf.

22. Ministerstwo Infrastruktury, *Strategia Rozwoju Transportu do 2020 roku (z perspektywą do 2030 roku). Główne kierunki w zakresie lotnictwa (projekt)*, Warszawa 2011.

23. Ministerstwo Transportu, *Program rozwoju sieci lotnisk i lotniczych urządzeń naziemnych*, Warszawa 2007.

24. Ministerstwo Transportu, Budownictwa i Gospodarki Morskiej, *Strategia Rozwoju Transportu do 2020 roku (z perspektywą do 2030 roku)*, Warszawa 2013, http://www.transport.gov.pl/files/0/1795904/130122SRTnaRM.pdf.

25. *Niebieska księga. Transport lotniczy*, new edition, version: 1.0, May 2008, http://www.funduszestrukturalne.gov.pl/NR/rdonlyres/B07E158E-3A7A-43A2-87C4-84E1533AA415/47155/BlueBookAirportsFinalDraftMRDMI12_092.pdf.

26. *Ochrona cywilnego ruchu lotniczego w Polsce, jako element bezpieczeństwa lotnictwa cywilnego. Informacja o wynikach kontroli*, 113/2012/P/11/062/KIN.

27. Organizacja Międzynarodowego Lotnictwa Cywilnego, *Podręcznik służb lotniskowych*, Doc 9137-AN/898, http://brama.pwsz.chelm.pl:2222/cgi-bin/libraopac. dll?bcd&sID= 0&hID=54601&lTyp=1.

28. *Plan generalny rozwoju i programu inwestycyjnego polskiego lotnictwa cywilnego. Streszczenie wykonawcze*, EER Systems Corporation, Vienna, Virginia 1992.

29. *Polska – podstawowe wielkości i wskaźniki w latach 1995–2010*, Ministerstwo Gospodarki, Warszawa 2011.

30. *Prognoza rozwoju transportu lotniczego w Polsce, Raport cząstkowy 2*, 22nd March 2010, Prepared on behalf of the Ministry of Infrastructure by the Gesellschaft für MKmetric Systemplanung,

31. http://siskom.waw.pl/komunikacja/lotnisko/CPL/analiza_2010/cpl_analiza_2010_raport_czastkowy_2.pdf.

32. Romański S., *Biała księga. Europejska polityka transportowa 2010: czas na podjęcie decyzji*, Wydawnictwo Naukowe Uniwersytetu Szczecińskiego, Szczecin 2002.

33. *Rynek lotniczy 2005: dynamika, wskaźniki, prognozy*, prepared by K. Łopaciński, Instytut Turystyki w Warszawie, "Wiadomości Turystyczne," Warszawa 2005.

34. *Rynek lotniczy 2006: dynamika, wskaźniki, prognozy*, prepared by T. Dziedzic, Instytut Turystyki w Warszawie, "Wiadomości Turystyczne," Warszawa 2006.

35. *Rynek lotniczy 2007: dynamika, wskaźniki, prognozy*, prepared by T. Dziedzic, Instytut Turystyki w Warszawie, "Wiadomości Turystyczne," Warszawa 2007.

36. *Rynek lotniczy 2008: dynamika, wskaźniki, prognozy*, prepared by T. Dziedzic, Instytut Turystyki w Warszawie, "Wiadomości Turystyczne," Warszawa 2008.

37. *Rynek lotniczy 2011: Air Transport Market 2011*, prepared by T. Dziedzic, Instytut Turystyki w Warszawie, "Wiadomości Turystyczne," Warszawa 2011.

38. *Rynek lotniczy 2012: Air Transport Market 2012*, prepared by D. Tłoczyński, Instytut Turystyki w Warszawie, "Wiadomości Turystyczne," Warszawa 2012.

39. *Rynek lotniczy w Polsce: przewoźnicy, przewozy, lotniska*, prepared by T. Dziedzic, K. Łopaciński, M. Więckowski, B. Radkowska, Instytut Turystyki, "Wiadomości Turystyczne," Warszawa 2003.

40. *Rynek lotniczy w Polsce. Raport Instytutu Turystyki '99*, prepared by T. Dziedzic, K. Łopaciński, Instytut Turystyki, "Wiadomości Turystyczne," Warszawa 1999.

41. Urząd Lotnictwa Cywilnego, Departament Rynku Transportu Lotniczego, *Analiza rynku transportu lotniczego w Polsce w latach 2004–2006*, Warszawa 2008, http://www.ulc.gov.pl/_download/wiadomosci/ 09_2008/analiza1.pdf.

42. Urząd Lotnictwa Cywilnego, *Główne kierunki rozwoju lotnictwa ogólnego w Polsce w latach 2007–2010*, Warszawa, August 2007, http://www.ulc.pl/_download/ opracowania/ starga0907.pdf.

43. Urząd Ochrony Konkurencji i Konsumentów, Departament Analiz Rynku, *Wpływ liberalizacji rynku połączeń lotniczych na konkurencję na tym rynku*, February 2010, www.uokik.gov.pl/download. php?plik=7914.

List of books

1. Assailly C., *Airport Productivity. An Analytical Study*, Institute of Air Transport, Paris 1989.
2. Baltagi B.H., *Econometric Analysis of Panel Data*, John Wiley & Sons, Chichester 2005.
3. Bednarczyk M., *Organizacje publiczne. Zarządzanie konkurencyjnością*, Wydawnictwo Naukowe PWN, Warszawa–Kraków 2001.
4. Bednarczyk M., *Otoczenie i przedsiębiorczość w zarządzaniu strategicznym organizacją gospodarczą*, Zeszyty Naukowe Akademii Ekonomicznej w Krakowie, Seria Specjalna: Monografie, Kraków 1996.
5. Bednarz R., Fletcher J., Gilbert D., Shepherd R., Wanhill S., *Principles Tourism and Practices*, Longman, London 1999.
6. *Benchmarking and Best Practices in Transport Sector*, eds. E. Marciszewska, J. Pieriegud, Oficyna Wydawnicza SGH, Warszawa 2009.
7. Bentkowska-Senator K., Kordel Z., *Transport w turystyce*, Wydawnictwo Uczelniane WSG, Bydgoszcz 2008.
8. Burnewicz J., *Wpływ członkostwa w Unii Europejskiej na transport w Polsce*, Urząd Komitetu Integracji Europejskiej, Warszawa 2003.
9. Cholewa A., *Koleje Dużych Prędkości w aspekcie rozwoju regionów Polski*, PKP PLK/RBF, seminar *High speed railways*, 14th November 2005.
10. Doganis R., Graham A., *The Role of Performance Indicators. Polytechnic of Central London*, Airport Management, London 1987.
11. Domańska A., *Wpływ infrastruktury transportu na rozwój regionalny*, Wydawnictwo Naukowe PWN, Warszawa 2006.
12. *Dostosowanie polskiego transportu do Unii Europejskiej. Współpraca i konkurencja transportu w poszerzonej Europie*, eds. D. Rucińska, E. Adamowicz, Wydawnictwo Uniwersytetu Gdańskiego, Gdańsk 2003.
13. Dutka A.F., *Competitive Intelligence for the Competitive Edge*, McGraw-Hill Professional, Chicago 2000.
14. *Ekonomika transportu*, ed. J. Burnewicz, Wydawnictwo Uniwersytetu Gdańskiego, Gdańsk 1993.
15. *Entrepreneurship in Tourism and Sport Business*, ed. M. Bednarczyk, Fundacja dla Uniwersytetu Jagiellońskiego, Kraków 2008.
16. Fleischer C.P., Bensoussan B., *Strategic and Competitive Analysis: Methods and Techniques for Analyzing Business Competition*, Prentice Hall, New York 2003.
17. Gierszewska G., Romanowska M., *Analiza strategiczna przedsiębiorstwa*, Polskie Wydawnictwo Ekonomiczne, Warszawa 2002.
18. Gorynia M., *Luka konkurencyjna na poziomie przedsiębiorstwa a przystąpienie Polski do Unii Europejskiej*, Wydawnictwo Akademii Ekonomicznej w Poznaniu, Poznań 2002.

19. Grabińska E., *Determinanty konkurencyjności regionalnego portu lotniczego*, Uniwersytet Jagielloński, Kraków 2014 (elaboration not published).

20. Graham A., *Airport Economics and Performance Measurement*, Airport Economics and Finance Symposium University of Westminster, London 1998.

21. Greene W.H., *Econometric Analysis. Sixth Edition*, Pearson, Prentice Hall 2008.

22. Grzelakowski A., *Polityka transportowa Unii Europejskiej i jej implikacje dla systemów transportowych krajów członkowskich*, Wydawnictwo Akademii Morskiej, Gdynia 2008.

23. Grzywacz W., *Polityka transportowa*, Wydawnictwo Naukowe US, Szczecin 1991.

24. Grzywacz W., *Rynek usług transportowych*, Wydawnictwa Komunikacji i Łączności, Warszawa 1980.

25. Hamel G., Breen B., *Managing tomorrow. What is your position in the future?* Harvard Business School Press, Red Horse Ltd., Cambridge 2008.

26. Hamel G., Prahalad C.K., *Przewaga konkurencyjna jutra. Strategie przejmowania kontroli nad branżą i tworzenia rynków przyszłości*, translation M. Albigowski, Business Press, Warszawa 1999.

27. *Handbook of Aviation Human Factors*, eds. D.J. Garland, J.A. Wise, V.D. Hopkin, Lawrence Erlbaum Associates, 1998.

28. Kahaner L., *Competitive Intelligence: How to Gather, Analyze, and Use Information to Move Your Business to the Top*, Simon & Schuster, New York 1997.

29. Kaliński D., *Zarządzanie organizacjami lotniczymi. Ekonomiczna charakterystyka usług lotnictwa cywilnego*, materiały szkoleniowe, Wydział Lotnictwa i OP Akademii Obrony Narodowej, Warszawa 2007.

30. Kaliński D., Marciszewska E., *Regionalny wymiar działalności portów lotniczych. Transport jako czynnik integracji regionów*, Fundacja na rzecz Uniwersytetu Szczecińskiego, Szczecin 2004.

31. *Kompendium wiedzy o konkurencyjności*, eds. M. Gorynia, E. Łaźniewska, Wydawnictwo Naukowe PWN, Warszawa 2010.

32. *Konkurencyjność małych i średnich przedsiębiorstw na polskim rynku turystycznym*, ed. M. Bednarczyk, Wydawnictwo Uniwersytetu Jagiellońskiego, Kraków 2006.

33. Koźlak A., *Ekonomika transportu – teoria i praktyka gospodarcza*, Wydawnictwo Uniwersytetu Gdańskiego, Gdańsk 2008.

34. Krabowiak H., *Podstawy infrastruktury transportu*, Wydawnictwo Wyższej Szkoły Humanistyczno-Ekonomicznej w Łodzi, Łódź 2009.

35. Kromer B., *System polskiego transportu w świetle integracji z Unią Europejską*, Wydawnictwo Uczelniane Politechniki Koszalińskiej, Koszalin 2004.

36. Kunert-Diallo A., *Kolizje praw w międzynarodowym transporcie lotniczym*, Lex a Wolters Kluwer business, Warszawa 2011.

37. Liberadzki B., Mindur L., *Uwarunkowania rozwoju systemu transportowego Polski*, Wydawnictwo Instytutu Technologii Eksploatacji – PIB, Warszawa–Radom 2007.

38. *Luka konkurencyjna na poziomie przedsiębiorstwa a przystąpienie Polski do Unii Europejskiej. Implikacje dla strategii firm i polityki gospodarczej*, ed. M. Gorynia, Wydawnictwo Akademii Ekonomicznej w Poznaniu, Poznań 2002.

39. *Marketing na rynku usług lotniczych*, eds. D. Rucińska, A. Ruciński, Wydawnictwo Uniwersytetu Gdańskiego, Gdańsk 2000.

40. Mendyk E., *Ekonomika i organizacja transportu*, Wyższa Szkoła Logistyki, Poznań 2002.

41. Murphy C., *Competitive Intelligence: Gathering, Analysing and Putting it to Work*, Gower Publishing, Aldershot 2005.

42. Neider J., *Transport międzynarodowy*, Polskie Wydawnictwo Ekonomiczne, Warszawa 2008.

43. Neider J., Marciniak-Neider, D., *Transport multimodalny w Europie*, Wydawnictwo Uniwersytetu Gdańskiego, Gdańsk 2005.

44. Perycz E., *Prognozowanie w transporcie*, Wydawnictwo WSE-I, Warszawa 2003.

45. Porter M.E., *Strategia konkurencji*, translation A. Ehrlich, Polskie Wydawnictwo Ekonomiczne, Warszawa 1992.

46. Porter M.E., *Strategia konkurencji, metody analizy sektorów i konkurentów*, translation A. Ehrlich, MT Biznes, Warszawa 2010.

47. Rasch G., *Probabilistic Models for Some Intelligence and Attainment Tests*, Danish Institute for Educational Research, Copenhagen 1960.

48. Rosik P., Szuster M., *Rozbudowa infrastruktury transportowej a gospodarka regionów*, Wydawnictwo Politechniki Poznańskiej, Poznań 2008.

49. Ruciński A., *Porty lotnicze wobec polityki otwartego nieba*, Fundacja Rozwoju Uniwersytetu Gdańskiego, Gdańsk 2008.

50. Strategor, *Zarządzanie firmą*, Polskie Wydawnictwo Ekonomiczne, Warszawa 2001.

51. Sweet K.M., *Aviation and Airport Security. Terrorism and Safety Concerns*, CRC Press, Boca Raton 2009.

52. *Transport. Problemy transportu w rozszerzonej UE*, eds. W. Rydzkowski, K. Wojewódzka-Król, Wydawnictwo Naukowe PWN, Warszawa 2009.

53. Truskolaski T., *Transport a dynamika wzrostu gospodarczego w południowo--wschodnich krajach bałtyckich*, Wydawnictwo Uniwersytetu w Białymstoku, Białystok 2006.

54. Tyrańska M., Walas-Trębacz, J., *Wykorzystanie metod analizy strategicznej w przedsiębiorstwie*, Wydawnictwo Uniwersytetu Ekonomicznego w Krakowie, Kraków 2010.

55. *Usługi portów lotniczych w Unii Europejskiej i w Polsce a prawo konkurencji i regulacje lotniskowe*, eds. F. Czernicki, T. Skoczny, Wydawnictwo Naukowe Wydziału Zarządzania Uniwersytetu Warszawskiego, Warszawa 2010.

56. Uszyński T., *Polskie prawo lotnicze z komentarzem*, Wydawnictwa Komunikacji i Łączności, Warszawa 1966.

57. Wells A.T., Chadbourne, B.D., *General Aviation and Management*, Krieger Publishing Company, 2002.
58. Wells A.T., Wensveen, J.G., *Air Transportation. A Management Perspective*, Brooks Cole, 2003.
59. Wells A.T., Young, S., *Airport Planning and Management*, McGraw-Hill Professional, New York 2003.
60. Williams G., *The Airline Industry and the Impact of Deregulation*, Ashgate, Adlershot 1993.
61. Wrzosek W., *Funkcjonowanie rynku*, Polskie Wydawnictwo Ekonomiczne, Warszawa 1994.
62. Zabłocki E., *Lotnictwo cywilne. Lotnictwo służb porządku publicznego*, Akademia Obrony Narodowej, Warszawa 2006.
63. Zając G., *Wspólna polityka lotnicza Unii Europejskiej*, Państwowa Wyższa Szkoła Wschodnioeuropejska w Przemyślu, Przemyśl 2009.
64. *Zarządzanie konkurencyjnością biznesu turystycznego w regionach*, ed. M. Bednarczyk, CeDeWu, Warszawa 2011.
65. Żabińska T., "Klastry turystyczne jako forma współpracy sieciowej i ich rola w budowaniu konkurencyjności regionu" [in:] *Konkurencyjność miast i regionów na globalnym rynku turystycznym*, ed. J. Sala, Polskie Wydawnictwo Ekonomiczne, Warszawa 2010.
66. Żylicz M., *Międzynarodowy obrót lotniczy. Zagadnienia ekonomiczno-prawne*, Wydawnictwa Komunikacji i Łączności, Warszawa 1972.
67. Żylicz M., *Prawo lotnicze międzynarodowe, europejskie i krajowe*, Wydawnictwo Prawnicze LexisNexis, Warszawa 2002.

List of articles

1. Albers, S., Koch, B., Ruff, C., "Strategic Alliances between Airlines and Airports – Theoretical Assessment and Practical Evidence," *Journal of Air Transport Management* 11, 2005.
2. Andrich D., "A Rating Formulation for Ordered Response Categories," *Psychometrika* 43(4), 1978.
3. Barbot C., "Low-cost Airlines, Secondary Airports, and State Aid: An Economic Assessment of the Ryanair-Charleroi Airport Agreement," *Journal of Air Transport Management* 12, 2006.
4. Barrett S., "Airport Competition in the Deregulated European Aviation Market," *Journal of Air Transport Management* 6, 2000.
5. Barros C.P., "Technical Change and Productivity Growth in Airports: A Case Study," *Transportation Research: Part A* 42, 2008.
6. Başar G., Bhat C., "A Parameterized Consideration Set Model for Airport Choice. An Application to the San Francisco Bay Area," The University of Texas at Austin, 2004.

7. Bednarczyk M., "Wpływ otoczenia komunikacyjnego na redefinicje strategii konkurencji polskich przedsiębiorstw" [in:] *Konkurencyjność przedsiębiorstw wobec wyzwań XXI wieku*, Wydawnictwo Akademii Ekonomicznej, Wrocław 1999.

8. Berbeka J., Borodako K., Klimek K., Niemczyk, A., Seweryn R., "An Analysis of Incentive Travel in Krakow in 2008–2009," *Zeszyty Naukowe Uniwersytetu Ekonomicznego w Krakowie* 2011.

9. Bernabei C., "Airports: an Integral Part of the Air Traffic Management System," *Air & Space Europe* 3(1–2), 2001.

10. Bojańczyk M., *Analiza pozycji firmy w konkurencyjnej gałęzi* [in:] *Przedsiębiorstwo rynek, konkurencja*, Szkoła Główna Handlowa, Warszawa 1995.

11. Boopen, S., "Air Access Liberalization and Tourism Development," *Journal of Travel & Tourism Research* 6(1), 2006.

12. Borenstein S., "Airline Merger, Airport Dominance and Market Power," *American Economic Review, Papers and Proceedings* 80, 1990.

13. Bruinsma F., "Comparative Study of Hub Airports in Europe. Ticket Prices, Travel Time and Rescheduling Costs," Free University Amsterdam, 1999.

14. Bryan D., O'Kelly M.E., "Hub and Spoke Networks in Air Transportation: an Analytical Review," *Journal of Regional Science* 39(2), 1999.

15. "Civil Aviation Authority, Catchment Area Analysis," *Working Paper*, October 2011.

16. Crouch G.I., "Modelling Destination Competitiveness: a Survey and Analysis of the Impact of Competitiveness Attributes," *CRC for Sustainable Tourism*, 2007.

17. Dobruszkes F. et al., "An Analysis of the Determinants of Air Traffic Volume for European Metropolitan Areas," *Journal of Transport Geography* 19, 2011.

18. Dreyer A., "Der Markt fur Kulturtourismus" [in:] *Kulturtourismus*, eds. A. Dreyer, Ch. Becker, München 2000.

19. Eisenkopf A., "Der intermodale Wettbewerbsrahmen der Verkehrspolitik," *Internationales Verkehrswesen* 3, 2005.

20. Forsyth P., "The Impacts of Emerging Aviation Trends on Airport Infrastructure," *Journal of Air Transport Management* 13, 2007.

21. Francis G., Humphreys I., Fry J., "The Benchmarking of Airport Performance," *Journal of Air Transport Management* 8, 2002.

22. Fuellhart K., "Airport Catchment and Leakage in a Multi-airport Region: The Case of Harrisburg International," *Journal of Transport Geography* 15, 2007.

23. Gilmour S.J., "Identification of Hospital Catchment Areas Using Clustering: An Example from the NHS," *Health Services Research* 45(2), 2010.

24. Goeldner, Ch.R., Ritchie B.J.R., *Tourism. Principles, Practcies, Philosophies*, 10th edition, JohnViley & Sons, New Jersey 2006.

25. Gorynia M., Jankowska B., Pietrzykowski M., Tarka P., Dzikowska M., "Przystąpienie Polski do strefy euro a międzynarodowa konkurencyjność i internacjonalizacja polskich przedsiębiorstw," *Ekonomista* 4, 2011.

26. Grabińska E., "Proces prywatyzacji przedsiębiorstwa turystycznego na przykładzie Orbis SA w aspekcie funkcjonującego rynku kapitałowego," *Zeszyty Naukowe Małopolskiej Wyższej Szkoły Ekonomicznej w Tarnowie* 10, 2007.

27. Grabińska E., "Rola i znaczenie regionalnych organizacji turystycznych w zakresie promocji turystycznej regionu" [in:] *Konkurencyjność miast i regionów na globalnym rynku turystycznym*, ed. J. Sala, Polskie Wydawnictwo Ekonomiczne, Warszawa 2010.

28. Grabińska E., "Socio-Demographic Profile of Tourists in Cracow," *Economics and Organization of Enterprise* 3(1), 2009, http://versita.metapress.com/content/k6517 m7319025873/fulltext.pdf.

29. Graham A., "Airport Benchmarking: a Review of the Current Situation," *Benchmarking: An International Journal* 12(2), 2005.

30. Graham, F., Humpreys, I., Fry, J., "The Benchmarking of Airport Performance," *Journal of Air Transport Management* 8, 2002.

31. Guan J.C. et al., "A Study of Relationship between Competitiveness and Technological Innovation Capability Based on DEA Models," *European Journal of Operational Research* 170, 2006.

32. Hakfoort J.R., Poort T., Rietveld R., "The Regional Economic Impact of an Airport: The Case of Amsterdam Schiphol Airport," *Regional Studies* 35(7), 2001.

33. Harumi I., Darin L., "Comparing the Impact of the September 11th Terrorist Attacks in International Airline Demand," *International Journal of the Economics of Business* 12, 2005.

34. Harvey G., "Airport Choice in a Multiple Airport Region," *Transportation Research* 21A, 6, 1987.

35. Hsiao C., "Analysis of Panel Data," Cambridge University Press, 2003.

36. Huang J.H., Peng, K.H., "Fuzzy Rasch Model in TOPSIS: A New Approach for Generating Fuzzy Numbers to Assess the Competitiveness of the Tourism Industries in Asian Countries," *Tourism Management* 33, 2012.

37. Huderek-Głapska S., "Wpływ portu lotniczego na rozwój gospodarki regionu," dissertation, Uniwersytet Ekonomiczny w Poznaniu, Poznań 2011.

38. Jarach D., "The Evolution of Airport Management Practices: Towards a Multi-point, Multi-service, Marketing-driven Firm," *Journal of Air Transport Management* 7, 2001.

39. Kamp V., Niemeier, H.M., *Benchmarking of German Airports – Some First Results and Agenda for Further Research*, www.gap-projekt.de.

40. Kamp V., Niemeier, H.M., Muller, J., "Can We Learn from Benchmarking Studies of Airports and Where Do We Want to go from Here," GARS Workshop on Benchmarking in Viena, November 2005.

41. Koch P.F., "Fractional Multinomial Response Models with an Application to Expenditure Shares," University of Pretoria, *Working Paper* 21, 2010.

42. Kowalczyk A., *Relacje zachodzące między rozwojem transportu lotniczego a rozwojem turystyki* [in:] *Współczesne uwarunkowania i problemy rozwoju turystyki,*: Institute of Geography and Spatial Management UJ, Kraków 2013.

43. Longhurst J., Gibbs, D.C., Raper, D.W., Conlan, D.E., "Towards Sustainable Airport Development," *The Environmentalist* 16(3), 1996.
44. Łatuszyńska M., "Metody badania wpływu infrastruktury transportu na rozwój społeczno-ekonomiczny regionu," *Problemy Ekonomiki Transportu* 1, 2007.
45. Marciszewska E., "Benchmarking jako instrument poprawy konkurencyjności działania na rynku lotniczym" [in:] *Współczesne problemy badawcze ekonomiki transportu*, Zeszyty Naukowe, nr 435, Ekonomiczne Problemy Usług, nr 3, Uniwersytet Szczeciński, Szczecin 2006.
46. Marciszewska E., Kaliński, D., "Port lotniczy jako czynnik rozwoju regionalnego" [in:] *Rozwój lotnictwa w regionach*, eds. A. Barski, W. Fabirkiewicz, Cz. Jarosz, Wydawnictwo Adam Marszałek, Toruń 2009.
47. Martin J.C., Roman, C., "A Benchmarking Analysis of Spanish Commercial Airports. A Comparison Between SMOP and DEA Ranking Methods," *Networks and Spatial Economics*, 6: DOI 10.1007/s11067-006-7696-1, 2006.
48. McLay P., Reynolds-Feighan, A., "Competition between Airport Terminals: The Issues Facing Dublin Airport," *Transportation Research: Part A* 40, 2006.
49. Morris J., Wilkinson, B., "The Transfer of Japanese Management Techniques to Alien Institutional Environments," *Journal of Management Studies* 32(6), 1995, http://mfiles.pl/pl/index.php/Just_in_time.
50. Nogalski B., Falencikowski, T., "Modele biznesów jako nowy obszar badań w naukach o zarządzaniu" [in:] *Nowe obszary badań w naukach o zarządzaniu*, ed. J. Rokita, GWST, Katowice.
51. Oum T.H., Yu, Ch., "Measuring Airports' Operating Efficiency: a Summary of the 2003 ATRS Global Airport Benchmarking Report," *Transportation Research: Part E* 2004.
52. Papke L.E., Wooldridge, J.M., "Econometric Methods for Fractional Response Variables with an Application to 401(k) Plan Participation Rates," *Journal of Applied Econometrics* 11(6), 1996.
53. Park Y., "An Analysis for the Competitive Strength of Asian Major Airports," *Journal of Air Transport Management* 9, 2003.
54. Park Y.H., "Applications of a Fuzzy Linguistic Approach to Analyse Asian Airports' Competitiveness," *Transportation Planning and Technology* 20, 1997.
55. Pitfield D.E., "The Economics of Airport Impact," *Transportation Planning and Technology* 7, 1981.
56. Sala J., "Porty lotnicze jako czynnik rozwoju turystyki w regionach (na przykładzie Międzynarodowego Portu Lotniczego im. Jana Pawła II w Krakowie-Balicach)" [in:] *Gospodarka turystyczna w regionie. Przedsiębiorstwo. Samorząd. Współpraca*, ed. A. Rapacz, Wydawnictwo Uniwersytetu Ekonomicznego we Wrocławiu, Wrocław 2011.
57. Starkie D., "Airport Regulation and Competition," *Journal of Air Transport Management* 8, 2002.

58. Tłoczyński D., "Skutki liberalizacji rynku usług transportu lotniczego dla regionalnych portów lotniczych" [in:] *Transport morski i lotniczy w obsłudze ruchu pasażerskiego*, ed. H. Salmonowicz, Wydawnictwo Naukowe Uniwersytetu Szczecińskiego, Szczecin 2005.

59. Wach K., "Mezootoczenie małych i średnich przedsiębiorstw w ujęciu czynnikowym," *Zeszyty Naukowe Uniwersytetu Ekonomicznego w Krakowie* 799, 2009, http://mpra.ub.uni-muenchen.de/31674/1/MPRA_paper_31674.pdf.

60. Walczak W., "Niematerialne determinanty konkurencyjności współczesnych przedsiębiorstw" [in:] *Konkurencyjność jako determinanta rozwoju przedsiębiorstwa*, eds. S. Lachiewicz, M. Matejun, Wydawnictwo Politechniki Łódzkiej, Łódź 2009.

61. Yoshida Y., Fujimoto H., "Japanese-airport Benchmarking with DEA and Endogenous-weight TFP Methods: Testing the Criticism of Overinvestment in Japanese Regional Airports," *Transportation Research Part: E 40* 2004.

Selected internet sources

ec.europa.eu
www.aci-europe.org
www.airportservicequality.aero
www.cie.gov.pl
www.cupt.gov.pl
www.dotacjeue.org.pl
www.easa.europa.eu
www.ec.europa.eu
www.eesc.europa.eu
www.eurocontrol.int
www.iata.org
www.icao.int
www.infor.pl
www.intur.com.pl
www.mi.gov.pl
www.mrr.gov.pl
www.transport.gov.pl
www.ulc.gov.pl

APPENDIX

LIST OF GRAPHS AND TABLES IN THE APPENDIX

Group A.2. Box plots for potential explanatory features of the model [graphs II–XVIII]

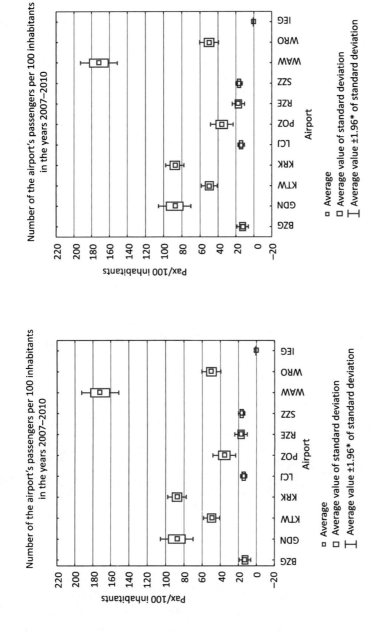

Number of the airport's passengers per 100 inhabitants in the years 2007–2010

□ Average
□ Average value of standard deviation
⊥ Average value ±1.96* of standard deviation

Graph II. Variable X1
Source: own study

Group A.1. Box plot for a dependent variable

Number of the airport's passengers per 100 inhabitants in the years 2007–2010

□ Average
□ Average value of standard deviation
⊥ Average value ±1.96* of standard deviation

Graph I. Box plot for a dependent variable Y
Source: own study

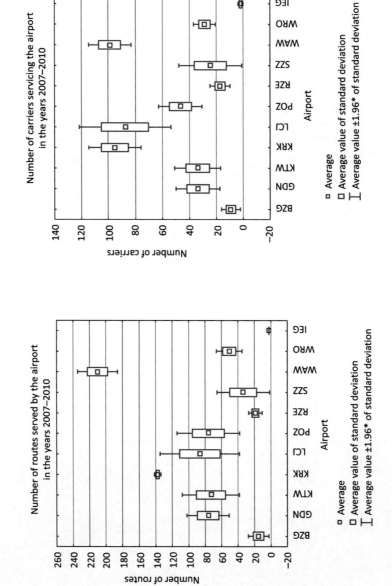

Graph III. Variable X2
Source: own study

Graph IV. Variable X3
Source: own study

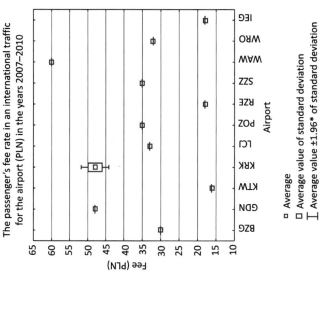

Graph V. Variable X4

Source: own study

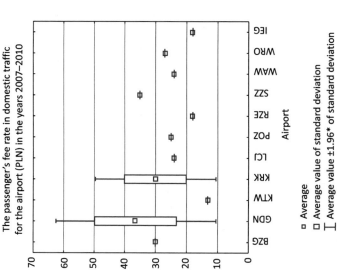

Graph VI. Variable X5

Source: own study

154

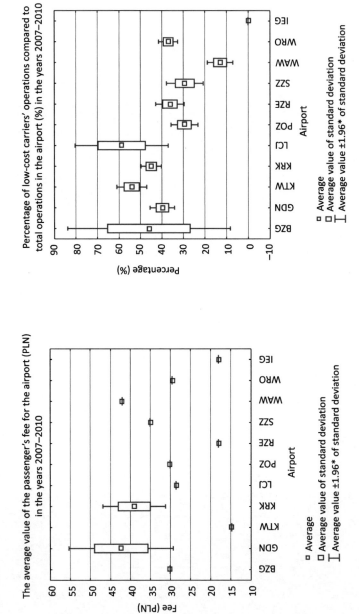

Graph VIII. Variable X7
Source: own study

Graph VII. Variable X6
Source: own study

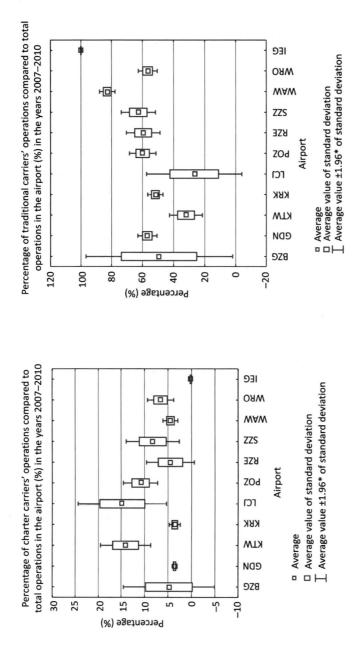

Graph X. Variable X9

Source: own study

Graph IX. Variable X8

Source: own study

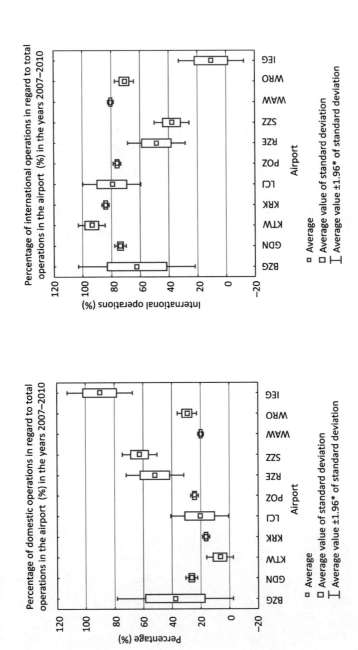

Graph XI. Variable X10

Source: own study

Graph XII. Variable X11

Source: own study

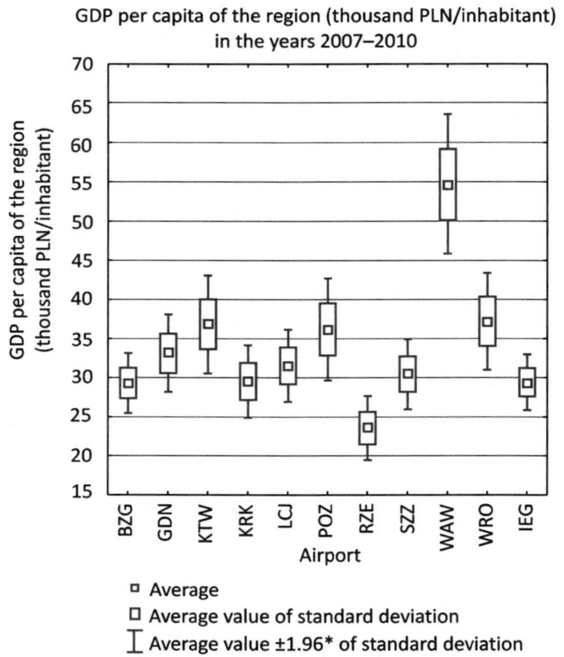

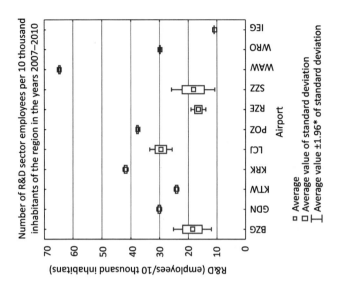

Graph XIV. Variable X13

Source: own study

Graph XIII. Variable X12

Source: own study

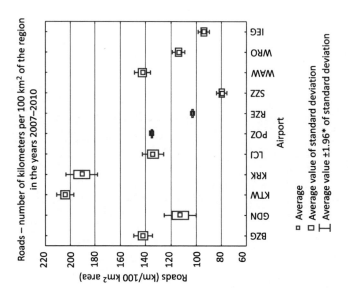

Graph XVI. Variable X15

Source: own study

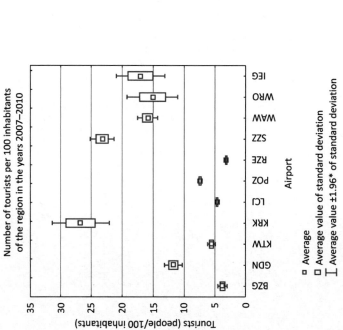

Graph XV. Variable X14

Source: own study

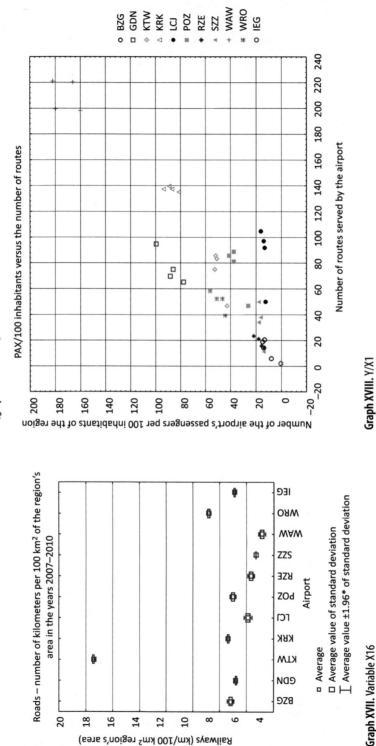

Group B. The box plot compiling dependent model variables including potential regressors [scatter charts: pax index/100 inhabitants indicator in regard to individual potential explanatory features [graphs XVIII–XXXII]

Graph XVIII. Y/X1
Source: own study

Graph XVII. Variable X16
Source: own study

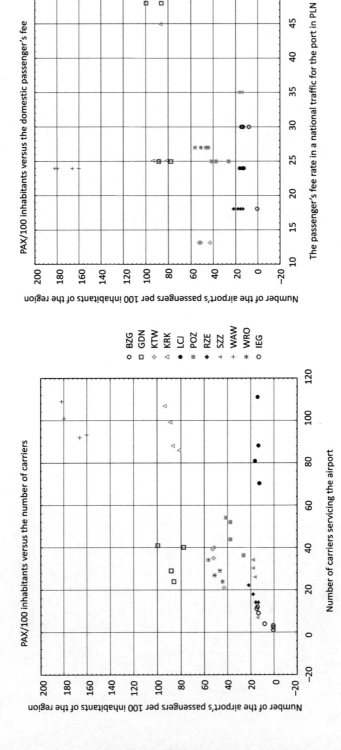

Graph XX. Y/X3

Source: own study

Graph XIX. Y/X2

Source: own study

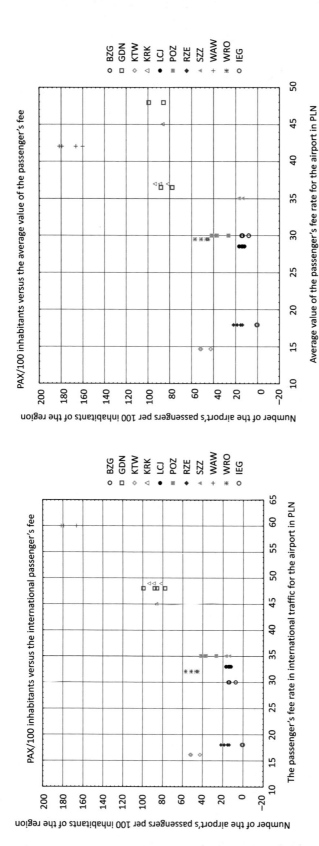

Graph XXII. Y/X5
Source: own study

Graph XXI. Y/X4
Source: own study

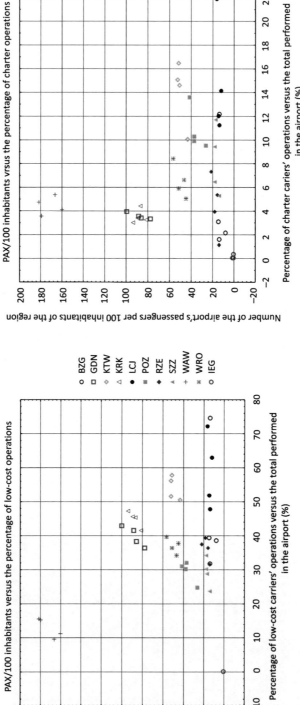

Graph XXIV. Y/X7
Source: own study

Graph XXIII. Y/X6
Source: own study

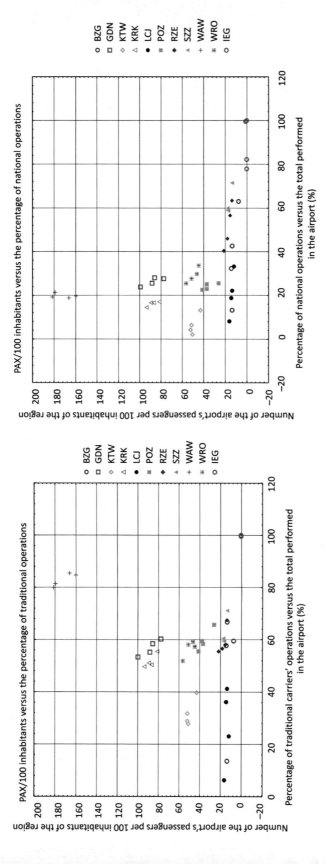

Graph XXVI. Y/X9

Source: own study

Graph XXV. Y/X8

Source: own study

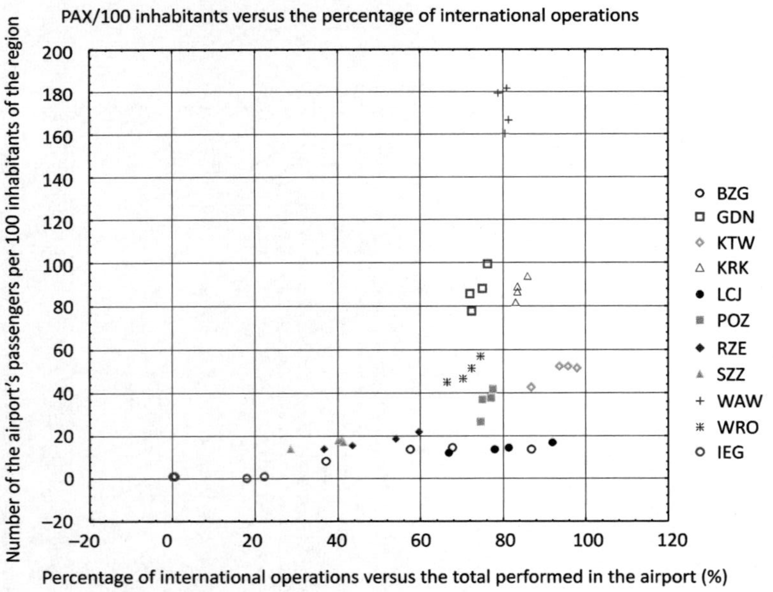

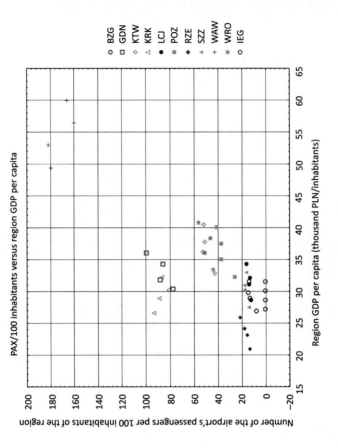

Graph XXVIII. Y/X11
Source: own study

Graph XXVII. Y/X10
Source: own study

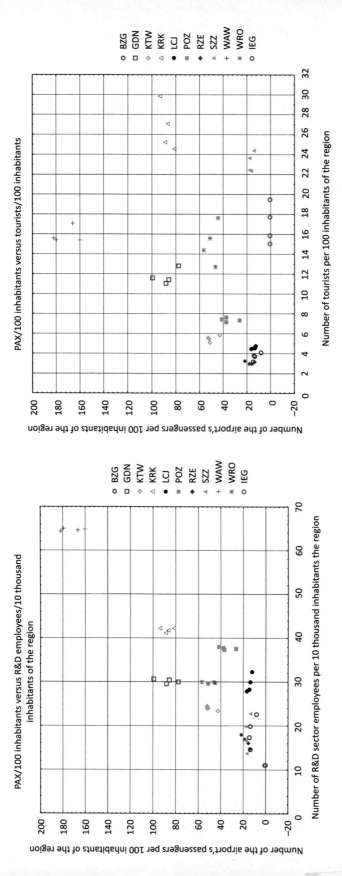

Graph XXX. Y/X13

Source: own study

Graph XXIX. Y/X12

Source: own study

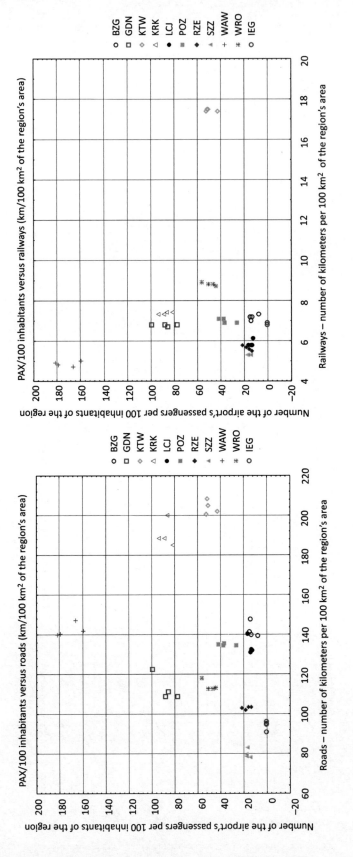

Graph XXXII. Y/X15
Source: own study

Graph XXXI. Y/X14
Source: own study

Group C. Table listing the observed values of the pax/100 inhabitants coefficient, and theoretical values, designated on the basis of fixed effects model for 11 Polish airports in the years 2007–2010

Table I. Scope of the estimated model: BZG AIRPORT:2007 – IEG AIRPORT:2010 (residual standard error = 3.92067)

	Λ pax_100_inhab. (empirical values)	Λ pax_100_inhab. (theoretical values)	Residuals
BZG AIRPORT:2007	7.6428	12.1153	−4.4724
BZG AIRPORT:2008	13.6469	11.9213	1.7256
BZG AIRPORT:2009	14.6938	11.5561	3.1377
BZG AIRPORT:2010	14.0279	14.4188	−0.3908
GDN AIRPORT:2007	77.6038	83.7540	−6.1502
GDN AIRPORT:2008	88.0453	86.4368	1.6085
GDN AIRPORT:2009	85.6717	86.6670	−0.9953
GDN AIRPORT:2010	99.6113	94.0743	5.5370
KTW AIRPORT:2007	42.7019	42.3298	0.3722
KTW AIRPORT:2008	52.2410	50.4458	1.7952
KTW AIRPORT:2009	50.9535	53.4482	−2.4947
KTW AIRPORT:2010	51.8403	51.5129	0.3273
KRK AIRPORT:2007	93.5702	89.3005	4.2696
KRK AIRPORT:2008	88.9516	87.5456	1.4061
KRK AIRPORT:2009	81.2645	86.5347	−5.2702
KRK AIRPORT:2010	86.5231	86.9286	−0.4055
LCJ AIRPORT:2007	12.1894	6.7301	5.4593
LCJ AIRPORT:2008	14.2750	14.5210	−0.2459
LCJ AIRPORT:2009	13.3876	14.3193	−0.9316
LCJ AIRPORT:2010	16.5208	20.8026	−4.2818
POZ AIRPORT:2007	26.4827	27.5835	−1.1008
POZ AIRPORT:2008	37.1867	41.0368	−3.8501
POZ AIRPORT:2009	37.3137	36.8657	0.4481
POZ AIRPORT:2010	41.5017	36.9988	4.5029
RZE AIRPORT:2007	13.4062	13.5248	−0.1186
RZE AIRPORT:2008	15.3914	15.3604	0.0310
RZE AIRPORT:2009	18.1969	19.3965	−1.1996
RZE AIRPORT:2010	21.5943	20.3072	1.2871
SZZ AIRPORT:2007	13.8100	13.3078	0.5022

	Λ *pax_100_inhab.* (empirical values)	Λ *pax_100_inhab.* (theoretical values)	Residuals
SZZ AIRPORT:2008	17.6565	18.2648	−0.6083
SZZ AIRPORT:2009	17.5004	21.1070	−3.6066
SZZ AIRPORT:2010	16.6840	12.9713	3.7127
PL WAW:2007	179.3430	174.4440	4.8996
PL WAW:2008	181.7780	177.2020	4.5759
PL WAW:2009	159.7400	166.0330	−6.2928
PL WAW:2010	166.1750	169.3570	−3.1827
WRO AIRPORT:2007	44.4867	48.4411	−3.9543
WRO AIRPORT:2008	51.0320	50.6926	0.3394
WRO AIRPORT:2009	46.7715	49.0767	−2.3052
WRO AIRPORT:2010	56.5694	50.6493	5.9201
7IEG AIRPORT:2007	0.6904	0.1208	0.5696
IEG AIRPORT:2008	0.5638	0.3979	0.1659
IEG AIRPORT:2009	0.3587	0.6338	−0.2751
IEG AIRPORT:2010	0.4554	0.9158	−0.4604

Source: own study.

Technical editor
Jadwiga Makowiec

Proofreader
Agnieszka Toczko-Rak

Typesetter
Hanna Wiechecka

Jagiellonian University Press
Editorial Offices: Michałowskiego 9/2, 31-126 Kraków
Phone: +48 12 663 23 81, +48 12 663 23 82, Fax: +48 12 663 23 83